HIDDEN GENIUS

Every owner of a physical copy of this edition of

HIDDEN GENIUS

can download the eBook for free direct from us at Harriman House, in a DRM-free format that can be read on any eReader, tablet or smartphone.

Simply head to:

ebooks.harriman-house.com/ hiddengenius

to get your copy now.

HIDDEN GENIUS

**The secret ways of thinking
that power the world's most
successful people**

POLINA MARINOVA POMPLIANO

HARRIMAN HOUSE LTD
3 Viceroy Court
Bedford Road
Petersfield
Hampshire
GU32 3LJ
GREAT BRITAIN
Tel: +44 (0)1730 233870

Email: enquiries@harriman-house.com
Website: harriman.house

First published in 2023.
Copyright © Polina Marinova Pompliano

The right of Polina Marinova Pompliano to be identified as the Author has been asserted in accordance with the Copyright, Design and Patents Act 1988.

Hardcover ISBN: 978-1-80409-003-9
eBook ISBN: 978-1-80409-005-3

British Library Cataloguing in Publication Data
A CIP catalogue record for this book can be obtained from the British Library.

CONTENTS

To Sofia,
Every moment with you
is extraordinary.
I love you.

INTRODUCTION

I DREADED HISTORY CLASS for as long as I can remember. Names, dates, places—it all felt like a jumbled jigsaw puzzle in my mind. Teachers often presented information as facts to be remembered, not rich personal stories of triumph, failure, risk, and regret. But as I made my way through the education system, I realized something important: Stories trigger emotion, and emotion triggers memory.

The only way I could retain information about a historical event was by reframing it as a story full of characters whose lives put everything in context. So rather than memorizing dates and events, I studied the lives of key players. What beliefs did they hold? What drove them to act in certain ways? What incentives were at play?

I learned about the French Revolution by investigating why people directed their rage at Marie Antoinette, a young queen who had become a symbol of excess and self-interest. I tried to imagine how she felt reading newspapers she believed mischaracterized and spread rumors about her. I felt a deep sense of sorrow when she lost custody of her young son who was forced to accuse her of various crimes. And, finally, I tried to imagine her humiliation, powerlessness, and terror as she approached the guillotine, walking to her death. What did she think in those last moments? What lessons had she learned during her short life?

Suddenly, the French Revolution wasn't just a historical event. It was a human story, full of grief, sadness, anger, desperation, and heartbreak—emotions we've all experienced at some point in our lives.

Without realizing it, I had stumbled upon something I like to call **people-focused learning**, the notion that people and their stories are at the center of any learning pursuit.

This type of learning goes beyond historical events.

If I want to improve my decision-making or develop mental resilience, I can choose a person who best embodies the idea about which I want to learn. From there, I'll immerse myself in their stories and begin searching for their "hidden genius," the differentiator that makes them truly exceptional. It could be a mental framework, a practical tidbit, or a timeless piece of wisdom that casts them as luminaries of their time.

So it was no surprise to anyone when I created a weekly newsletter called **THE PROFILE** in February 2017. It features a range of *profiles*, or long-form articles that delve into the detailed story of an individual. My newsletter has been read by tens of thousands of people—including actor Dwayne "The Rock" Johnson, famed restaurateur Danny Meyer, and my wonderful mom.

But to me, **THE PROFILE** is the physical manifestation of how I learn. So even if I wasn't writing a newsletter, I'd still be reading profiles and learning from the life paths of those who have built something meaningful, developed a useful way of thinking, and—most importantly—helped others unlock their own hidden genius.

I'm not the only one who subscribes to the people-focused

learning style. Some of the world's most successful people discovered their own hidden genius by first studying the genius of those who came before them.

The late basketball legend Kobe Bryant says that when he was a young player he went to "G.O.A.T. Mountain" (an acronym for "Greatest Of All Time") to speak to players like Magic Johnson, Michael Jordan, Larry Bird, Jerry West, Oscar Robertson, and Bill Russell. He asked them, "What did you do? What were your experiences? What was the process like for you?"

Similarly, before Steve Kerr got the head coaching job with the Golden State Warriors, he decided to visit all the coaches he greatly admired. He met with legends including Phil Jackson, Gregg Popovich, Lute Olson, Lenny Wilkens, and Pete Carroll. Kerr wanted to understand the nuts and bolts of what made them so great.

Kerr had a seemingly contradictory but profound breakthrough: He realized that he wasn't going to be successful if he idolized his mentors. "The main theme that came across over and over again in these conversations was, be yourself," he says. "There's no point in trying to be someone else. You can *emulate* somebody else, but you can't *be* someone else."

Before you read the coming pages, I want to be clear what this book is *not*. It is not a compilation of traditionally successful people who are portrayed as unblemished "heroes" worthy of worship. This book is about *learning,* not *idolizing.*

Take world chess champion Magnus Carlsen as an example. Carlsen was only 13 years old when he became a grandmaster, so interviewers loved to ask him about his idols. He explained that he had learned a lot from players including Vladimir Kramnik, Garry Kasparov, and Bobby Fischer—but he didn't idolize a single one of them.

"It's never really been my style, according to my philosophy, to idolize players, to try to copy them. I just try to learn and get the best from the great masters, contemporary and from the past," he says. Taking the best *from* the best—rather than blindly imitating them as one-for-one models—allowed Carlsen to develop his own strengths and style.

After studying and interviewing so many remarkable figures, I don't envy or hero-worship any of them. I have seen that success doesn't exist in a vacuum—people are dealing with family drama, money problems, insecurities, and all sorts of human messiness on a daily basis.

Al Pacino may be considered one of the most iconic actors that's ever lived, but he's had a pretty tumultuous personal life. At age 81, Pacino has three children but he's never been married, a choice that likely stems from his early experience with his own parents, who divorced when he was only two years old. Pacino is self-aware enough to know that he's given up certain things along the way in order to fulfill professional goals.

Remember, if you could follow in the exact footsteps of someone who has achieved the upper echelons of success in your field, would you? While reading this book, I encourage you to ask yourself: Am I willing to make the same sacrifices, the same missteps, the same trade-offs? With the good comes the bad.

If there's one thing I've discovered after years of learning about people it's this: A person's life is never linear. It looks more like a winding, tangled web of ups and downs than it does a straight, predictable line. No matter what life serves up, however, we can almost always extract lessons about what to replicate *and* what to avoid.

Keep in mind this important distinction: Idolizing traps you into imitating "perfect" versions of imperfect people. Learning, on the other hand, allows you to observe, synthesize, and pave your own path.

This book will expose you to the hidden genius of a wide

variety of people whose journeys have taught them practical lessons you can apply to your own life if you so choose. There is no perfect human being, but I believe that we can all learn from each other's most fulfilling successes—as well as our most devastating failures.

The people featured in this book will offer tools to help you boost your creativity, strengthen your relationships, and improve your decision-making. I invite you to come with me on a learning journey that will ultimately lead you to discover your own hidden genius.

Chapter One

UNLEASHING YOUR CREATIVE POTENTIAL

THINK ABOUT THE most creative person you know. What makes them so?

For centuries, we've mistakenly attributed creativity to factors outside of our control. You may hear it referred to as a talent, a gift, or some sort of inexplicable genius that few people possess.

But in reality, creativity is a skill. And like any other skill, it can be learned. Creativity is simply the ability to generate fresh ideas, think of new ways to solve old problems, and create original work.

We understand this conceptually, but what does creativity look like in practice?

In my years of studying people with creative minds, one name comes to mind: Grant Achatz. He's a revolutionary chef who lost his sense of taste and still built the number-one restaurant in the world.

Through his story, I learned that we've got creativity all wrong. Ideas are not hard to come by, breakthrough creative acts often masquerade as massive failures, and success is frequently creativity's silent killer.

"I often say that being creative is simply being aware of your surroundings, and translating these impulses into a specific medium," Achatz once wrote. "For me, that medium is cooking and dining."

Through his food, Achatz has been able to elicit curiosity, surprise, wonder, and bewilderment in his guests. Here's how his story—paired with those of other creative geniuses—can help us unleash our own creative potential.

MAKING A CONNECTION

Imagine that you sit down to dine at Achatz's Chicago-based restaurant Alinea. Immediately, you notice that things aren't as they seem.

You forgo plates to eat directly off a tablecloth resembling a large-scale painting. You pick up a tomato only to realize it tastes like a strawberry. Your dessert is a floating edible balloon.

That's because dinner at Alinea isn't really dinner—it's a performance filled with elements of magic and mystery that's designed to mesmerize the guest each night.

This experience is made possible because the restaurant's creator Grant Achatz asked himself the question: Who says food can't be art?

Achatz is considered one of the most creative and cutting-edge chefs in America. His creativity stretches far beyond his elaborate and non-conventional dishes—it begins the second a guest walks into Alinea's false-perspective hallway.

Achatz founded Alinea—named the best restaurant in the world by luxury travel magazine *Elite Traveler* in 2018—almost 20 years ago. Alinea is one-third laboratory, one-third sensorium, and one-third theater. A guest is served anywhere between 17 to 19 courses, a meal structure that echoes the effect of chapters in a book. Alinea's most iconic dishes over the years include a pillow of nutmeg air, a black truffle explosion, and an edible helium-filled floating balloon.

Achatz infuses elements of surprise, texture, flavor, and aroma to challenge the guest's taste experience and trigger their emotions. It sounds more like magic than cooking—and that's by design.

"We treat the emotional component of cooking food as a seasoning," Achatz says in an episode of the Netflix series *Chef's Table*. "You add salt, you add sugar, you add vinegar, you add nostalgia. If you're able to move people, then it's not just about having dinner—it's about something more."

That "something more" often stems from the bizarre ideas swirling around in Achatz's brain. How does he generate such unconventional ideas? By seeing the world through "a kaleidoscope of food."

In other words, his ideas come from the most unlikely sources—it could be while listening to a song on the radio, watching leaves fall to the ground, or seeing a large-scale painting in a museum. "You're constantly bombarded with ideas, and it's up to us to figure out a way to translate them to our guests," he says.

One time, he was listening to the rock band Rage Against the Machine, wondering why that style of music kept him so engaged. As he processed the peaks and valleys of the tempo, he asked himself, "How can I break the monotony of the dining experience?" He began crafting a tasting menu whose progression mirrored a Rage Against the Machine song's movement from low points to steep climaxes.

Another time, a customer entered Alinea's kitchen to thank Achatz for a dish he had prepared that night. As she was talking, Achatz zoned in on her dangling, red-beaded earrings. That same night, he took out a sheet of paper and sketched out an idea for a new dish—he wanted to create an edible string with touches of something red.

Because Achatz frequently borrows ideas from other

disciplines, Alinea transforms into an entirely new restaurant every four months. New menu, new decor, new experiences. This is baked into the DNA of the restaurant—the name Alinea originates from the Latin phrase *a linea*, which refers to the start of a new paragraph. The restaurant's name is meant to symbolize "the beginning of a new train of thought."

As sexy as it sounds, Achatz's idea-generating process is not new.

In the 1500s, Renaissance artist Leonardo da Vinci used a similar process he called "connecting the unconnected," which meant finding relationships between two totally unrelated subjects.

He would sometimes throw a paint-filled sponge against the wall and contemplate the shapes of the stains to try and find new ideas in them.

Most notably, he was standing by a well and noticed a stone hit the water at the same moment that a bell went off in a nearby church tower. Leonardo noticed the stone caused circles until they spread and disappeared.

By simultaneously concentrating on the circles in the water and the sound of the bell, he made the connection that led to his discovery that sound travels in waves.

Leonardo discovered that the human brain naturally forms relationships between two disparate inputs, no matter how dissimilar. In other words, if you focus on two subjects for a period of time, you will see relationships and form connections that trigger new ideas.

Leonardo said, "It should not be hard for you to stop sometimes and look into the stains of walls, or ashes of a fire, or clouds, or mud or like places, in which you may find marvelous ideas."

This sort of divergent thinking that Leonardo Da Vinci describes is supported by neuroscience research. Roger E. Beaty is the author of *The Creative Brain* and the director of the

> *It should not be hard for you to stop sometimes and look into the stains of walls, or ashes of a fire, or clouds, or mud or like places, in which you may find marvelous ideas.*

LEONARDO DA VINCI

Cognitive Neuroscience of Creativity Lab at Pennsylvania State University. He has conducted various behavioral experiments while using brain imaging to measure creativity.

In one such experiment, he gave participants pairs of randomly selected words, such as "shoe" and "door" or "rowboat" and "parrot," while asking them to rate just how connected those two words were to each other. The more creative the person, the more they were able to see connections between unrelated items.

Beaty went on to say that the common ingredients for creativity—whether you're a scientist or an artist—include "flexibility of thinking, the ability to make connections."

As another modern creative genius named Steve Jobs said in a 1996 *WIRED* interview: "Creativity is just connecting things. When you ask creative people how they did something, they feel a little guilty because they didn't really *do* it, they just *saw* something. It seemed obvious to them after a while. That's because they were able to connect experiences they've had and synthesize new things."

CHRISTOPHER NOLAN,
Director of Inception, Memento, *and* The Dark Knight Trilogy

The structure of film director Christopher Nolan's films follows a musical framework called the "Shepard tone," a series of ascending notes on a scale. It's an auditory illusion in which the tone gives an impression of an infinitely rising pitch. You've heard it in pretty much every Nolan film, but you've also experienced it in the narrative. "I wanted to try to apply it to screenwriting," he says. "Can you braid together the three storylines in such a way that you create the idea of a continuing rise in intensity?"

DOMINIQUE CRENN,
Chef and owner of Atelier Crenn

For restaurateur Dominique Crenn, ideas for new dishes "always come from outside the kitchen." She's generated ideas by walking around a museum, taking a stroll in the woods, or lounging by the side of the pool. One time, she was walking her dogs in Buena Vista Park in San Francisco with a friend while they discussed an impending state ban on foie gras, paté made from the livers of force-fed geese and ducks. Crenn said she then saw a bird's nest in a tree. She knew that she needed to start over without using foie gras. She conceived of a dish that would use her leftover foie gras supply as the dirt, corn silk to make the nest, and corn pearls to make bird eggs. She would title it, "Birth," to represent a new beginning.

Pay attention to the world around you—the next great idea may be hiding in plain sight.

MANUFACTURING CREATIVITY

People used to say creativity came from God. Today they talk about the "muse" (a phrase that remains steeped in divinity, deriving from the Ancient Greek "Muses" or goddesses of inspiration).

But, as Stephen King wrote in his memoir, *On Writing*, "There is a muse, but he's not going to come fluttering down into your writing room and scatter creative fairy-dust all over your

There is a muse, but he's not going to come fluttering down into your writing room ... He lives in the ground. He's a basement guy. You have to descend to his level.

STEPHEN KING

typewriter or computer screen. He lives in the ground. He's a basement guy. You have to descend to his level, and once you get down there, you have to furnish an apartment for him to live in." In other words, the muse, the divine, the magic—it's stuff we make up to avoid the grunt work that comes with being creative.

As Achatz pushed the boundaries of the culinary world, Alinea became recognized as the best restaurant in the world. He felt fulfilled and gratified. He was living the dream he'd had since he was ten years old.

And then the unthinkable happened. In 2008, Achatz was diagnosed with stage-four tongue cancer. Alinea's genius chef had lost his ability to taste. "There was a light bulb that went off and said, 'For the first time ever, I think I can be a chef without being able to taste.' Because it's up here," he says, pointing to his head. "It's not here," he adds, pointing to his mouth.

Could that be true? Could it be that you can *think* your way to creativity? Without the ability to taste, Achatz had no choice but to test it out.

He came up with a technique called "flavor bouncing." He takes a sheet of paper and draws a big circle around one central, thematic ingredient. He calls this the "focal ingredient" that will set the tone for the entire dish. Then he bounces "satellite ingredients" (or complementary ingredients) off the focal ingredient by drawing lines to each one.

The whole idea of this creative method is that the central ingredient has to complement all the supporting ingredients, and each supporting ingredient must complement at least one other supporting ingredient. This way, there isn't a rogue, clashing ingredient that throws off the flavor profile of the entire dish.

For instance, let's say the focal ingredient is white beans. What goes with white beans? He'll make a circle for "bacon." He'll make another circle for "apple." And another for "maple syrup."

When he makes one for "beer," Achatz's internal dialogue goes like this:

"Does a Guinness go with white beans? Sure, everyone drinks beer with their pork and beans."

"Does beer go with maple syrup? Absolutely. They make some beer with maple syrup."

"Does beer go with apples? Of course, you can drink beer with apples."

"And does beer go with bacon? Well, everything goes with bacon, so of course, beer goes with bacon."

What if he added red wine? That wouldn't go with a number of the satellite ingredients, so it would be considered a clashing element.

The drawing ends up looking like a bunch of satellites orbiting Earth. It's a creative method rooted in logic.

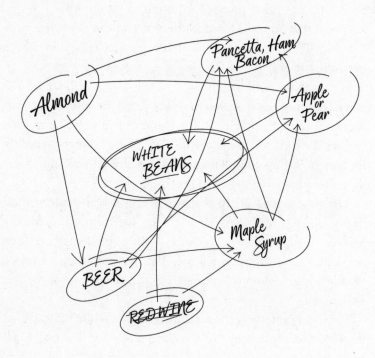

People like to think the creative process is romantic. ... The truth, for me at least, is that creativity is primarily the result of hard work and study.

GRANT ACHATZ

The cancer diagnosis forced Achatz, a chef who couldn't taste, to figure out new ways to keep Alinea at the forefront of culinary innovation. As someone who makes a living by creating a new tasting menu every couple of months, Achatz cannot afford to wait for his muse to arrive. In turn, he dismantles the notion that the world's greatest creators have an innate "gift" for creativity.

Creativity is less a fleeting moment of inspiration and more a muscle that can be trained through consistent exercise. "People like to think the creative process is romantic," Achatz says. "The artist drifts to sleep at night, to be awakened by the subliminal echoes of his or her next brilliant idea. The truth, for me at least, is that creativity is primarily the result of hard work and study."

AARON SORKIN,
Screenwriter, director, and playwright

Aaaron Sorkin believes that rules augment creativity. But there's a slight nuance: You need to *understand* the rules, not necessarily *follow* the rules.

His bible for storytelling is Aristotle's *Poetics*, which outlines the rules of drama. It may sound counterintuitive to look to rules and structure for creative inspiration, but here's Sorkin's reasoning: Once you learn what elements are typically present in every film, only then can you deconstruct them, play with them, and rearrange them.

In other words, you can break the rules only when you know the rules. As Sorkin says, art is beautiful because of its basic adherence to some set of rules, while finger painting is the result of complete unstructured freedom.

SHONDA RHIMES,
Showrunner, executive producer, and writer

———

Shonda Rhimes is behind some of the most addictive shows on TV: *Grey's Anatomy*, *Scandal*, and *How to Get Away With Murder*.

Her hidden genius is that she's figured out how to manufacture *and* scale creativity. For Rhimes, the creative process begins with a single line of dialogue in her head. Before she ever writes it down or shares it with others, she lets it simmer in her mind for some time.

"I never put pen to paper to write the script or book or anything until I really know what I'm going to write," she said at the Summit LA17 conference in Los Angeles. "And then the writing is quick: Sometimes it can take a year of me thinking, and I can then write a script in three days."

Scientists call this process "creative incubation," referring to the process your brain undergoes after it's introduced to a problem (such as a potential plot line). Research shows that the brain unconsciously works to find solutions to the problem even when your attention is occupied by other tasks. This helps explain why many people experience flashes of creativity while doing rote activities such as exercising, showering, or driving.

FAILING INTO SUCCESS

What does it mean to create original work? I'm talking about the groundbreaking, mind-exploding, revolutionary kind.

I attended a conference in 2019 where writer Tim Urban

gave the keynote speech. In it, he explained just how hard it is to create original work in the face of conventional wisdom. "When you're trying to create something truly original, you make a bunch of mistakes," he said. "Originals are a mess."

Urban also wrote a four-part deep-dive on entrepreneur Elon Musk (you know, the guy trying to create a clean energy future, colonize Mars, and prevent robots from becoming our overlords).

Here's how Urban characterized the difference between the way Musk thinks and the way most people think. It's the difference between a chef and a cook. "When I say chef, I don't mean any ordinary chef," Urban writes. "I mean the trailblazing chef—the kind of chef who *invents* recipes. And everyone else who enters a kitchen—all those who *follow* recipes—is a cook."

The chef reasons from first principles, whereas the cook works off some version of a recipe that's already out there.

Although Achatz is in a radically different industry, he and Musk have a lot in common. They both *invent* the recipes other people follow.

But here's the catch about doing something truly original: It's sometimes messy, which makes it vulnerable to criticism—especially by incumbents.

One week after Alinea opened its doors, the *New York Times* published a review of the restaurant. A fellow chef referred to Achatz and several of his peers as doing work that he considered to be "child's play" and "nonsense upon stilts." The *Times* food critic said Alinea's four-and-a-half-hour dining experience was exhausting and its cuisine could be "pointlessly weird."

Achatz's reaction was unexpected.

"The very first thing I do is immediately assume whoever is criticizing me is right," he told *Esquire* in 2015.

Why? "Nobody likes to be told that they don't do something well. I don't care who you are—if you say otherwise, then you're just flat out lying. But at the end of the day, you need to have enough confidence in yourself and in your team to look at it objectively." The act of simply considering that a fraction of criticism may be accurate will keep you learning, unlearning, fixing, tweaking, generating new ideas—and, ultimately, gaining respect.

But the question remains: How can we produce work that's not only original but truly disruptive?

Let's take a look at someone who revolutionized the animation industry.

Ed Catmull, who had a doctorate in computer technology, co-founded animation film studio Pixar alongside Steve Jobs and John Lasseter in 1986, and the trio began taking creative risks that shook up the world of entertainment.

Catmull's hidden genius lies in his ability to use both sides of his brain, the creative and the logical. In his five-decade career, Catmull helped bring to life a number of computer-animated hit films, including *Toy Story, Finding Nemo, Ratatouille, Wall-E,* and *Inside Out.* As a computer scientist, he also invented algorithms, made important discoveries in computer graphics, and helped pioneer digitally realistic films.

Perhaps counterintuitively, Catmull credits his grand success to his consistent willingness to fail. When asked how Pixar's animation units manage to pull off one hit after another, he says: "If something works, you shouldn't do it again. We want to do something that is new, original—something where there's a good chance of failure [each time]."

He believes the big, juicy failures are where true, groundbreaking originality lies. During the creative process, Catmull encourages his team to experiment, fail, and learn over and over again until the film reaches their desired level of quality.

Catmull's greatest, most practical piece of advice is this: "Aim to fail the 'elevator test.'"

The moment we graduate from college, we're told we need

to perfect our "elevator pitch," the ability to convey an idea to higher ups in a 30-second elevator ride.

Catmull says if you can pass the elevator test, your idea is probably derivative of what's been done before. In other words, it's not as original as you think.

Truly ambitious ideas—"a rat that wants to cook," or "an old man who floats away on a balloon with a stowaway"—can't be summed up in 30 seconds, but they *can* go on to become the Oscar-winning Pixar films *Ratatouille* and *Up*, respectively.

Original creators typically have three characteristics in common: They have a unique point of view on the world. They are confident they can achieve an ambitious goal. And finally, they are willing to fail spectacularly in the name of creating something revolutionary.

"Initially, the films we put together, they're a mess. It's like everything else in life—the first time you do it, it's a mess," Catmull says. "Sometimes it's labeled 'a failure' but that's not even the right word to use. It's just like, you get the first one out, you learn from it, and the only failure is if you don't learn from it, if you don't progress."

TAYLOR SWIFT,
Singer-songwriter

Imperfections can turn regular work into an original masterpiece. Whether it's art, movies, or books, people talk more about the flawed things that get stuck in their heads than they do the obvious, perfect things. Artist Taylor Swift understands this better than most. After she released her song, 'Blank Space,' people kept mishearing her lyric, *"Got a long list of ex-lovers"* as *"All the lonely Starbucks lovers."* Swift inadvertently benefited from the imperfection in the song—the flaw made it memorable and led people to talk about it with their friends. The song was number one on the charts for nine weeks in a row.

CHRISTINA TOSI,
Founder of Milk Bar

Christina Tosi, the creator of dessert sensation Milk Bar, is big on tinkering. She plays with texture, flavor, taste, and smell. Tosi's mind has been described as "fiercely analytical and precise," allowing her to approach her work like a scientist.

She observes, hypothesizes, tests, and analyzes until she finally gets to a particular flavor profile. It takes hours—and sometimes days—to reach a level of perfection deemed worthy of Tosi's standards. Tosi says you need to fail *at least* 40 times in the pursuit of a goal before you even get close to success.

But it's important to note one can tinker too much as perfectionism is a common pitfall of creatives. At a certain point, you have to stop fixing and adjusting and put it out into the world for feedback. And sometimes *her* idea of perfection isn't the same as her customers' idea of perfection. She says, "So much of what we learn happens in the mistakes. It doesn't happen in the perfect moments."

Bits of
GENIUS

Creativity arises from making new connections— contemplate unexpected things together.

Don't wait for moments of inspiration to strike. Creativity is a muscle; exercise it.

There's a logic to creativity: find what works for you, break it down, and you have a process that can serve you forever.

Unstructured freedom is the enemy of true creative achievement. Find and learn the rules—you can break them afterwards.

Rote activities can provide creative incubation. Your brain works on solutions while your body is occupied with other tasks.

True creativity is impossible without being open to failure. Don't think in terms of elevator pitches; embrace risk.

Embracing risk in creativity can require a degree of mental toughness, of course. But there are some creative ways to master mental toughness, too, as we'll see in the next chapter.

Chapter Two

MASTERING MENTAL TOUGHNESS

MENTAL TOUGHNESS IS an elusive thing. Is it a mindset? Can it be achieved without undergoing severe stress and trauma? Why does it seem like some people have it and others don't?

What exactly is it that links ultra-runners, Navy SEALs, and Holocaust survivors?

The definition of mental toughness varies depending on who you ask, but one commonality is the **ability to endure**.

And enduring pain, discomfort, and uncertainty for long periods of time doesn't happen by accident. In this chapter we're going to meet people who have mastered the art of staying calm in chaotic and emotionally taxing situations. Many of them have been through hell, and they've emerged as more resilient and confident versions of their previous selves.

But how?

MANUFACTURING HARDSHIP

David Goggins was in his early 20s, suffering from asthma, a learning disability, a stutter, and crushingly low self-esteem, when an evening on the couch began an unexpected journey.

"The most important conversation you'll ever have is the conversation you have with yourself—and my conversation was absolutely horrifying.

DAVID GOGGINS

You could call it "Couch-to-4,000 pull-ups." It ultimately saw him endure three Navy SEAL Hell Weeks, more than 50 endurance races, and obtain the world record for most pull-ups in 24 hours (4,030 to be precise).

Goggins wasn't in a great place when the breakthrough came. And the breakthrough itself came from a pretty unexpected source.

He had recently returned to civilian life after a stint with the Air Force where he aimed to become a pararescue specialist: a highly trained operator who acts as a parachutist, scuba diver, or rock climber to conduct some of the most difficult rescue missions. After failing the swimming component of the program, Goggins dropped out of pararescue school and got a job as a pest control technician.

He returned home from his $1,000-a-month job spraying for cockroaches with a 42-oz shake from Steak 'n Shake. Then he sat down in front of the TV and began channel-surfing.

"I saw this show on the Discovery Channel," says Goggins. "It was just guys going through Hell Week [the brutal Navy SEALs training exercise]. They were freezing, there was a lot of water, and it brought back memories of me going through pararescue training. So at 297 pounds, I decided to try to be a Navy SEAL."

Goggins began by signing up for endurance races in order to get physically fit. But he soon discovered that his body was only half the battle—his mind also needed work.

Growing up, Goggins had lived in fear. At school, he experienced incessant bullying and racism. At home, he suffered physical and emotional abuse at the hands of his father.

"The most important conversation you'll ever have is the conversation you have with yourself—and my conversation was absolutely horrifying," Goggins says. "I thought I was dumb. I was a nobody. I was a loser."

He carried these insecurities with him in his 20s. He only

confronted them for the first time when he signed up for the Badwater 135, a race that requires participants to run 135 miles in 24 hours in the peak heat of Death Valley.

To qualify, Goggins had to first run a 100-mile race in San Diego, but he had never run long-distance before. The result? Goggins peed blood, nearly passed out, broke the bones in his feet, and endured stress fractures—but he finished the race.

"This was the worst pain I had been in in my entire life," he told podcaster Joe Rogan. "But at mile 81, something clicked. My mind knew I wasn't fucking around anymore. It knew it wasn't going to quit. It was me against me. And I used all these different dark places to start bringing out light. And I started going deeper and deeper."

This was the race that taught Goggins he needed to develop mental tools to endure pain.

His first tool came from the Navy. **He dubbed it "The 40% Rule."** The rule is the reason why even though most people hit a wall at mile 20 during a marathon, they're still able to finish.

It's simple: When your mind is telling you that you're done, that you're exhausted, that you cannot possibly go any further, you're probably only actually 40% done.

"A lot of cars have governors on them at, let's say, 91 miles an hour," explains Goggins. "It may only go 91 miles an hour because the governor stops it from going 130. We do the same thing to our brain. When we get uncomfortable, our brain gives us a way out—usually quitting or taking the easier route."

The second tool Goggins used is what he calls the **"accountability mirror."** It's a way of undergoing controlled emotional pain.

When Goggins decided to become a Navy SEAL, he looked at his reflection and said, "You're fat, you're lazy, and you're a liar. What are you going to do about it?"

This sounds harsh, but Goggins says that he needed to face his insecurities in order to overcome them. And the second half of that statement—the focus on remedies—made it something more than self-criticism. He pasted sticky notes around the outside of the mirror outlining the steps he needed to take to achieve his goals.

They would say things like, "Go one day without lying for external validation" or "Go on a 2-mile run."

Third, Goggins decided to **do something that sucks every single day**—because suffering begets growth. Often, that means acting against your first instinct. It's pouring rain outside? Go run anyway. Your house is a mess but you're tired? Clean it anyway.

This way of thinking puts you on the offensive and gets you out of lazy, comfortable routines. "I brainwashed myself into craving discomfort," Goggins adds.

Needless to say, suffering is rarely voluntary. We normally experience pain and suffering against our will: When a loved one dies, a relationship falls apart, or we unexpectedly lose our job. And if you haven't put yourself through some voluntary suffering—or "callused your mind," as Goggins would say—then you're in for a wild ride.

But you can do that. Think of it as **stress-testing** yourself.

You can artificially manufacture hardship. And by creating some intentional friction in your life, your mind will be better prepared for heavy experiences you may have to endure in the future.

Navy SEALs are particularly proficient at manufactured hardship. SEAL training teaches candidates the difficult task of gaining control over their physiology. They use a principle called "The Four Pillars of Mental Toughness," which includes goal-setting, mental visualization, positive self-talk, and arousal control.

Arousal control—intentionally regulating your emotional response—is the most interesting because it's a skill very few people possess. When the average person is under intense duress, they start sweating, their heart starts racing, and the mind goes blank. But SEALs learn how to override the body's natural responses in the most extreme circumstances.

For example, Navy SEALs' heart rates remain steady when they are engaged in combat, and athletes describe a state of tunnel vision and effortless excellence in high-pressure situations.

"The Buddha famously said that life is suffering," Goggins writes. "I'm not a Buddhist, but I know what he meant and so do you. To exist in this world, we must contend with humiliation, broken dreams, sadness, and loss. That's just nature. Each specific life comes with its own personalized portion of pain. It's coming for you. You can't stop it. And you know it."

And this is the reason that Goggins believes it's imperative you not only manufacture hardship but *seek it out* on a daily basis. Choosing the path of most resistance builds authentic confidence. Many of us, Goggins says, want the results without the process. We forget that pain is necessary to make progress.

TOMMY CALDWELL,
Rock climber

Rock-climber Tommy Caldwell says the best thing his dad did was expose him to "elective hardship." As a young kid, the father-son duo got caught in blizzards, slept in snow caves, and climbed massive mountains.

"I have spent years pondering why some manage to harness trauma for the better while others flounder," Caldwell says. "I think my best theory to date is that it comes down to the training. Adventure is the best adversity training I know of."

Victimhood is optional ... We become our own jailers when we choose the confines of the victim's mind.

EDITH EVA EGER

EDITH EVA EGER,
Psychologist and Holocaust survivor

"Suffering is universal," Holocaust survivor Edith Eva Eger writes in her memoir *The Choice*. "But victimhood is optional."

We're all likely to be victimized in some way throughout the course of our lives. At some point, we will suffer some kind of affliction or abuse, caused by circumstances or people over which we have little or no control. "This is victimization," she writes. "It comes from the outside. It's the neighborhood bully, the boss who rages, the spouse who hits, the lover who cheats, the discriminatory law, the accident that lands you in the hospital."

On the flipside, *victim*hood comes from the *inside*. No one can make you a victim but you. "We become victims not because of what happens to us but when we choose to hold on to our victimization. We develop a victim's mind—a way of thinking and being that is rigid, blaming, pessimistic, stuck in the past, unforgiving, punitive, and without healthy limits or boundaries. We become our own jailers when we choose the confines of the victim's mind."

If you don't give in to victimhood, you can develop a kind of mental resilience that will carry you through the most difficult situations.

PERSONIFYING PAIN

Can you become immune to pain?

Most of us are conditioned to think we need to avoid pain at all costs. But what happens if you personify pain and see it as a friend rather than an adversary?

Dubbed "The Queen of Pain," Amelia Boone is a corporate attorney at Apple by day and an obstacle endurance racer by night.

She signed up for her first Tough Mudder race at age 28 when she realized she couldn't do a single pull-up. A Tough Mudder is an endurance race in which participants attempt to complete miles-long obstacle courses, which typically include swimming through ice water, making your way through dangling wires that give off an electric shock, and squeezing through a labyrinth of pipes.

After that she became obsessed with getting stronger, and went on to become a three-time World's Toughest Mudder champion and one of the most decorated obstacle racers in history—all while working full time at Apple.

To find time for training outside of the regular workday, Boone began waking up at 4 am and hitting the trails for several hours of running, before getting to the office by 7.

In 2019, Boone ran Big's Backyard Ultra, an infamous event (often described as "sadistic") in which runners complete a 4.167-mile loop over and over again, until there's one person left standing.

"I love the mental aspect of racing, and so much of [Big's Backyard Ultra] was mental," she tells me. "It's very much just about focusing on getting through that next loop in front of you."

When the pain levels began to feel insurmountable, Boone knew that if she lost control of her mind, she would inevitably lose control of her body. So she used the technique of **"making friends with pain."**

"I don't ever want to see pain as an adversary. Pain is your friend. Pain gives you cues. Pain tells you what you need to focus on," she says. "During races, I'll literally talk to different body parts: 'OK foot, you kind of hurt right now.' If I personify pain, I can think of it as separate from me. And if I make friends with it, then it is just something there to guide me—and teach me."

Another endurance athlete who personifies pain is ultra-runner Courtney Dauwalter.

In 2017, she dominated the headlines after she won the Moab 240, a 240.3 mile footrace through some of Utah's most challenging terrain. It took her 58 hours, and she beat the second-place finisher by more than ten hours.

Dauwalter has managed to stay calm even through bouts of severe nausea, a bleeding head injury, and temporary blindness. "I don't think those types of pain and suffering are signs you should stop," she told sports writer Sarah Barker. "I mean, I troubleshoot and try to fix what's causing it, but my solution is usually to just keep going."

Dauwalter has conditioned herself into thinking about pain as a **place**: She visualizes herself entering "the pain cave." Sometimes, you enter "the pain cave" voluntarily and other times life shoves you in there against your will.

The reason it's helpful to personify pain is that it serves as a reminder that you're in control when you enter and equally as aware that you can leave. "It's not a place I'm scared to enter," she says. "It's a place I'm excited to find the entrance to."

When I interviewed mental performance coach Lauren Johnson, she told me there's an important distinction between listening to yourself and talking to yourself. You should avoid the former and encourage the latter.

When you *listen* to yourself, you hear all the negativity and all the reasons why you can't go on, she says, but when you *talk* to yourself, you can tell yourself the things you need to hear in order to overcome the challenge ahead of you.

Goggins is an expert at self-talk, and he's convinced himself that pain is a gatekeeper that holds the key to the greatest things in life. "Pain," he says, "unlocks a secret doorway in the mind, one that leads to both peak performance, and beautiful silence."

Masters of suffering don't see pain as discomfort or torture that happens to them. They see it as a living being that lets their mind in on the secret that takes them to the next level.

PETER SCOTT-MORGAN,
Roboticist dubbed
"the human cyborg"

After he was diagnosed with Lou Gehrig's disease, Peter Scott-Morgan did something radical—he became a cyborg. Scott-Morgan merged his humanity with artificial intelligence and robotics to create a lifelike avatar of his former self. What does this mean?

He reached out to several companies that would help create a synthetic voice that sounded like his own, an animated 3D avatar, and an eye-tracking system that would allow him to communicate.

He sees this degenerative disease—and the emotional and physical pain that comes with it—as a bully. And he knows how to deal with bullies. Scott-Morgan has been with his husband since 1979, and they became the first gay couple whose marriage was legally recognized in Britain. "When

Fear, to a great extent, is born of a story we tell ourselves, and so I chose to tell myself a different story.

CHERYL STRAYED

we were younger," Scott-Morgan says, "we were bullied by the police, the boys at school, by Margaret Thatcher and her government. Society as a whole didn't value us. We learned from experience that you stand up to bullies; you don't let them see you're hurting."

In their eyes, Lou Gehrig's disease is the biggest bully they've encountered so far. By framing the disease as a bully, it gives Scott-Morgan fuel to keep fighting.

CHERYL STRAYED,
Author

In 1995, Cheryl Strayed was a 26-year-old waitress whose life hit rock bottom after she lost her mother to cancer just a few years prior. As her life began to spiral out of control, she decided to hike the Pacific Crest Trail—a wilderness trail that runs all the way from Mexico to Canada.

During her trek, she confronted all sorts of pain and fear. When darkness began to descend on the trail, Strayed's imagination began playing tricks on her. She would hear sounds and see shadows that made her heart race. She was constantly scanning the path for rattlesnakes, mountain lions, and serial killers. And then one day, she realized that if she let fear overtake her, the journey was doomed.

So she began talking to herself, asking the question: "Who's going to be your ruler?" Would it be fear? Pain? Anxiety? Courage?

She chose bravery. Strayed didn't see another human being for the first eight days of her hike, but she began to personify her aloneness. "Alone had always felt like an actual place to me, as if it weren't a state of being, but rather a room where I could retreat to be who I really was," she writes in her memoir *Wild*. "The radical aloneness of the PCT had altered that sense."

It took her 94 days to walk 1,638 miles, often completely alone. Two days before her 27th birthday, she reached her destination. "Fear, to a great extent, is born of a story we tell ourselves, and so I chose to tell myself a different story from the one women are told," she writes. "I decided I was safe. I was strong. I was brave. Nothing could vanquish me."

DEVELOPING AN ALTER EGO

If you ever spend time with David Goggins, or watch him in conversation, you'll notice something unusual from time to time.

He sometimes refers to himself in the third person.

This isn't an accident. Nor is it arrogance. Instead, it's part of a deliberate strategy to create a separate identity that distances him from his past of bullying, fear, and abuse.

"I had to create 'Goggins,'" he explains, "because 'David Goggins' was a weak kid. I wanted to be proud of who I was."

Goggins likes to say he was built, not born.

Adopting an alter ego is an extreme form of "self-distancing," a psychological tool that helps people reason more objectively and see the situation from a slight distance.

Immersing yourself in your feelings can lead to unhealthy mental rumination, so creating a little bit of distance from the self can help us better regulate our emotions. One way people can create a temporary alter ego is through **illeism**—the act of referring to oneself in the third person.

Illeism is not generally well received. It makes the subject sound grandiose. But it can be a powerful tool for reducing anxiety and building confidence. "There are studies that show when people talk about previous traumatic events in the third person, they tend to regard themselves through much more compassionate eyes," says psychotherapist Kim Schneiderman.

Self-distancing is also a helpful strategy in helping us manage our emotions better. "When you create an alter ego, it actually feels like we have a choice, and we're not identifying with who we are in that very moment but that we have a choice to be who we want to be," says mental performance coach Lauren Johnson. "When we distance slightly, we give ourselves the ability to choose."

A distanced perspective can help soothe anxiety and fear by allowing us to muster confidence for the moments that matter. Here's the cool part: In the beginning, your core self and your alter ego may seem like two disparate entities. But eventually they begin to blend together.

So over time, David Goggins came to fully embody his alter ego "Goggins." "I sought out pain, fell in love with suffering, and eventually transformed myself from the weakest piece of shit on the planet into the hardest man God ever created, or so I tell myself," he says.

But don't be fooled—athletes aren't the only masters of suffering.

Take, for example, Anthony Ray Hinton. Unlike Goggins, Boone, and Dauwalter, Hinton wasn't seeking out pain. Thanks to a flawed justice system, pain was inflicted upon him much against his will.

In 1985, Hinton was arrested and wrongfully charged with two counts of capital murder in Alabama. Hinton knew it was a case of mistaken identity and naively believed that the truth would prove his innocence and set him free.

Instead Hinton, a poor black man in the South, was sentenced to death by electrocution. He maintained his innocence through the entire 30 years he served on death row, making him one of the longest-serving death row prisoners in Alabama history.

Hinton underwent mental, emotional, and physical duress every day of his life for three decades. He watched 54 men walk past his cell to be executed. Another 22 took their own lives. "My cell was 30 feet from the chamber, and I could smell the burning flesh," he writes in his memoir *The Sun Does Shine*.

Hinton harnessed the power of his mind to escape the brutal reality of being alone 24 hours a day. In solitary confinement, many people have mental breakdowns, give up, and commit suicide. How did he keep himself sane all these decades?

He did something radical. Hinton escaped the prison cell without ever leaving solitary confinement. How? He turned his pain into a daydream in which he could assume alter egos that distanced him from the label of "lifelong prisoner."

While confined in his cell, Hinton could create different identities for himself: He became a world traveler, husband to Halle Berry, guest to the Queen of England, and even winner of Wimbledon—all in his mind. "I never used my mind for garbage," he says. "I used it to cope through some lonely days."

The point is that you're not permanently tethered to the identity you currently have—you can alter it to get closer to the person you want to become. As author James Clear writes, "Your current behaviors are simply a reflection of your current identity. What you do now is a mirror image of the type of person you believe that you are (either consciously or subconsciously)."

Goggins transformed from a victim into one of the world's toughest athletes. He *became* his alter ego. But how?

"First, you have to face the real you. The real me is David Goggins—I stutter, I have these issues with reading and writing, and I'm fat and insecure. You have to face that in that dark room," he says. "In that dark room is who you are, but in that dark room is where you have to create another human being. In the dark room, you face yourself, you realize you want to be better, you realize you don't want to be this insecure, weak person you were who has all these problems we all have."

These places—Goggins's dark room, Dauwalter's pain cave, and Hinton's solitary confinement cell—serve as places of metamorphosis. You go in as one type of person, undergo unimaginable pain and suffering, and come out the other side with a new sense of self.

If you don't break, you'll transform. As Goggins says, "Life will always be the most grueling endurance sport, and when you train hard, get uncomfortable, and callus your mind, you will become a more versatile competitor, trained to find a way forward no matter what."

BEYONCÉ KNOWLES,
Singer-songwriter

Early in her career, Beyoncé was shy and reserved—far removed from the powerhouse people would see on stage. She created an alter ego she called "Sasha Fierce" that allowed her to perform with a level of confidence she herself didn't yet have.

"I'm not like her in real life at all," Beyoncé said in 2006. "I'm not flirtatious and super-confident and fearless like her." As you can imagine, Beyoncé doesn't need the crutch of an alternate persona to get through her performances anymore. She's become confident just being herself. "Sasha Fierce is done. I killed her," Beyoncé told *Allure* in 2010. "I don't need Sasha Fierce anymore, because I've grown, and now I'm able to merge the two."

KOBE BRYANT,
NBA All-Star

———

Kobe Bryant was known for his "Black Mamba" alter ego. It was a way to get through the lowest point of his career. The nickname was inspired by the movie *Kill Bill*, in which the snake, known for its agility and aggressiveness, was used as a code name for a deadly assassin.

"The length, the snake, the bite, the strike, the temperament," he said. "That's me!"

At a time when people were chanting "Kobe sucks," while he was playing, Bryant said that using an alter ego gave him emotional distance from his real self. "I was able to switch my mind to something else," he says. "When I make the mental switch [to the Black Mamba], I know it's 'go time.'"

FRANK ABAGNALE,
Ex-con man

———

Frank Abagnale was an airline pilot, a doctor, a U.S. Bureau of Prisons agent, a sociology professor, and an attorney—all before he was 21 years old. How did he do all of this? He put on a uniform, assumed a fake identity, and earned the trust of the people in charge.

People often refer to Abagnale as the greatest con man of all time.

"A man's alter ego is nothing more than his favorite image of himself," Abagnale writes in his memoir *Catch Me If You Can*. "The mirror in my room in the Windsor Hotel reflected my favorite image of me—a darkly handsome

A man's alter ego is nothing more than his favorite image of himself.

FRANK ABAGNALE

young airline pilot, smooth-skinned, bull-shouldered, and immaculately groomed."

Everyone can access this alternate version of themselves, and Abagnale did it by playing dress-up. Your clothes and demeanor can signal status, wealth, and even physical attraction. "I learned early that class is universally admired," Abagnale says. "Almost any fault, sin or crime is considered more leniently if there's a touch of class involved." A con artist impersonates to *deceive*, while a confident person impersonates to *become*.

Bits of GENIUS

You're tougher than you think. When your mind is telling you that you're finished, that you're exhausted, that you cannot possibly go any further, you're probably only actually 40% done.

Self-criticism can become self-destructive. Instead seek self-accountability—honesty combined with a focus on practical remedies.

Stress-test yourself through regular manufactured hardship.

Remember that victimhood is always optional.

Make friends with pain. It tells you what you need to concentrate on. And by personifying it, you separate it from you. It can teach you.

Avoid listening to yourself. Start talking to yourself.

Self-distancing—such as using an alter-ego—can help you be more objective about your situation.

Metamorphosis awaits those who can be honest about their situation without breaking.

Toughness is essential to human flourishing—but you can't flourish without strong relationships with other people, as we'll see next.

Chapter Three

UNL CKING HEALTHY RELATI NSHIPS

MY HUSBAND AND I got married in July 2020 at the height of the coronavirus pandemic. The only other people in attendance were the minister and the photographer.

After I said my vows, I thought about all the people who had told me, "Your life will never be the same once you get married." And if there's one thing I've learned after three years of marriage, it's that the idea that marriage changes everything is kind of a myth.

Sure, you're now legally bound to each other, but your partnership remains largely unchanged. Your conflict-resolution strategies are the same. Your communication patterns are the same. Your general outlook on life is the same.

To optimize for a great partnership, though, all of those things need to evolve in the long run. As the pandemic showed us, relationships of all kinds can become strained. Marital and workplace conflicts have been on the rise, with people's stress levels exacerbated by unpredictable economic ups and downs.

So it's only natural that in today's modern and ultra-connected world, we're experiencing higher levels of uncertainty, crippling self-doubt, and relational anxiety.

Relationships play a key role in nearly every aspect of our lives. Whether it's our spouse, our child, our parents, our teacher, our boss, our customer, or our business partner—we're all entangled in a web of human connection. As renowned couples therapist Esther Perel likes to say, "The quality of our relationships determines the quality of our lives."

As you'll discover in this chapter, there are relationship "masters" and "disasters." Let's examine the secret ways of thinking the masters use to nurture healthy, fulfilling relationships.

THE COMPOUND INTEREST OF TRUST

Name a relationship in your life where you trust someone who is inconsistent. You can't. That's because we can't rely on people—whether in work, business, or family—who repeatedly break their promises.

Trust is the bedrock of any relationship. It's built out of long-term consistency, commitment, and communication. And we need it more than ever. Esther Perel is a psychotherapist who has devoted her life to coaching couples through all the intricacies of intimacy and connection.

Every day, couples all over the world grapple with interpersonal problems—infidelity, work stress, and financial pressures. So what do we do to lessen those unpleasant feelings?

We seek comfort, connection, and most importantly, trust. "In archetypal language you could say that once we're thrown out of Eden, we are on a quest for trust, for that solid ground, for that sense that tomorrow will arrive when today ends," Perel says.

What if I told you there is a formula for earning trust?

First, let's explore the situations in which trust breaks down.

In our society, infidelity is often used to represent the ultimate breach of trust and lack of respect in a relationship. But what people don't realize is that there are countless other things they do to chip away at their partnerships.

"People cheat on each other in a hundred different ways: indifference, emotional neglect, contempt, lack of respect, years of refusal of intimacy," Perel says. "Cheating doesn't begin to describe the ways that people let each other down."

Contrary to the common refrain, "Trust takes years to build and seconds to break," most relationships don't collapse because of one blowout fight. They often fall apart because the partners have eroded the foundation of trust over *a long period of time.*

Here's the thing: Trust cuts across the familial *and* the collegial. If you're dating a new partner, you need to figure out if you can rely on them to build a healthy relationship. If you're an investor, you need to be able to evaluate whether a founder is trustworthy before you invest your money in their company. In both cases, you're optimizing for the long term, but how can you build trust with the limited and incomplete information that you have today?

Entrepreneur and investor Naval Ravikant believes that "All returns in life, whether in wealth, relationships, or knowledge, come from compound interest."

Compounding growth happens when an asset's earnings—such as interest—generate additional earnings over time. Long-term efforts, Ravikant explains, aren't just good for compounding interest, they're also effective for compounding trust in situations of "goodwill, or love, or relationships, or money." The more you invest in a relationship, the more "trust" interest it pays.

The long game often appears boring, but the longer that you play it, the more profound the effects. And it's a double-edged sword—repeat the negative and you'll get more negative, repeat the positive and you'll get more positive. They *both* have the power to compound.

The more consistent the action, the faster the compounding. In other words, the two key ingredients for trust are time and

> *If your proposed marriage contract has 47 pages, my suggestion is you not enter.*

CHARLIE MUNGER

consistency. LinkedIn founder Reid Hoffman says the formula for earning trust is as follows:

$$Trust = Consistency + Time$$

In simple terms, it goes like this: If you consistently do what you say over a long period of time, then trust is inevitable. As time goes by, the goodwill between the two partners will compound at a faster rate.

The result? Mutual trust.

Mutual trust allows you to make decisions, seal deals, and enjoy relationships without constantly questioning the other person's motives. "If I'm doing a deal with someone I've worked with for 20 years and there is mutual trust, we don't have to read the legal contracts," Ravikant says. "Maybe we don't even need to create legal contracts; maybe we can do it with a handshake."

Speaking of contracts, compound interest was popularized by legendary investors Warren Buffett and Charlie Munger. Munger believes that the highest form a civilization can reach is a seamless web of deserved trust. There isn't a ton of control, strict rules, or paranoia.

"Not much procedure," he says, "just totally reliable people correctly trusting one another. That's the way an operating room works at the Mayo Clinic."

What you want in your life, he says, is to build a web of deserved trust among reliable people. "And so," he says, "if your proposed marriage contract has 47 pages, my suggestion is you not enter."

TOBI LÜTKE,
Founder of Shopify

Tobi Lütke says it's not useful to think that trust is mostly binary—you either trust someone or you don't. It's much more complex than that, and he uses the metaphor of a "trust battery" to explain it.

When you enter into a personal or professional relationship with someone, your trust battery starts at roughly 50%, and every interaction you have with the person either charges or discharges the battery a little bit. "Just like with your phone, if the battery is low, you think all the time about the battery," he says. "It's the same with people. Those who are low on trust, you think of all the time. The people who are high on trust, you don't worry about as much."

Aim to be a person whose trust battery stays consistently charged at over 80%.

JOHN GOTTMAN,
Psychologist

John Gottman believes that "sliding door moments" build, maintain, or crumble the foundations of trust in our relationships. (The "sliding door" terminology comes from the Gwyneth Paltrow movie *Sliding Doors*, where her two lives play out in parallel after she makes—or misses—her train.)

These moments are the seemingly inconsequential things we haphazardly throw back and forth at each other on a daily basis. What does your partner do when you reach out to hold their hand? Or when they see you are visibly upset? Do they ignore you and turn away or do they lean in and respond with empathy? "Each moment is not that important," he says, "but if you're always choosing to turn away, then trust erodes in the relationships very gradually, very slowly."

DEFUSING CONFLICT

Esther Perel has a secret about marital arguments: The form often precedes the content. In other words, we tend to follow a pretty strict formula regardless of what we're arguing about.

"If you argue a certain way, it doesn't matter if you're talking about money, sex, your parents, or breakfast. Every conversation will look alike," she says. "One of you starts to raise your voice; the other rolls their eyes. One goes up a notch; the other walks away. It's a dance often organized by the vulnerability cycle."

Perel often cites the work of couples researcher Howard Markman, who found that people tend to listen for only about ten seconds before they tune out and mentally begin forming their rebuttal.

We *hear*, she says, but we do not *listen*.

One person who knows a thing or two about listening is former hostage negotiator Chris Voss. As the FBI's lead international kidnapping negotiator, he spent 24 years of his career mastering the art of listening. In fact, people's lives depended on it.

In 1993, two men held three employees hostage at a Chase Manhattan Bank in Brooklyn, New York. Voss was the second negotiator on the phone.

As he begins talking to one of the bank robbers, he identifies himself and immediately begins employing several strategies during the conversation.

First, he manipulates the tone of his voice because Voss believes this is the most important tool during a negotiation. He uses a technique he calls **"The Late Night FM DJ" voice**, a declarative, soothing, and downward-inflecting voice that is applicable in nearly every situation.

The reason it's effective is because it hits the mirror neurons in your counterpart's brain and triggers a neurochemical reaction that calms them down. In turn, it creates an involuntary response of clearheadedness in both parties. "Genuine curiosity is a hack for emotional control," he says. "If you talk out loud in a smooth, calming voice, you can actually calm yourself down."

Next, Voss begins "mirroring" the hostage-taker by repeating his statements as questions. When the bank robber says, "You guys chased my driver away," Voss responds with, "We chased your driver away?" **Mirroring** is an effective technique that can be used to build goodwill and gather information. You "mirror" someone by repeating several key words they used in their last communication. (i.e: "I had a really hard day because of all the stress I'm under." Response: "The stress you're under?") It's a useful tool because it keeps you emotionally sober while allowing the other person to continue talking.

Finally, he begins labeling. He tells the second bank robber, "It wasn't your fault, was it?" and "You regret this happened, don't you?" Both of these questions insinuate he got roped into a bad situation. **Labeling** is used to verbally identify and name your counterpart's emotions. A good label would be responding with one of the following: "It seems like... It looks like... You seem to be..." (e.g., "It seems like you're in a stressful situation.")

Using both mirroring and labeling in the same conversation defuses negative feelings, ensures the other person feels heard, and allows you to better understand the context of the other person's feelings.

Mastering these three skills can help you sharpen one of the most important skills in any relationship: emotional intelligence. The reason Voss was able to get the bank robbers to surrender and free the hostages is because he did what most of us don't do in the midst of a high-pressure conflict—he *listened*.

In turn, the negotiating tools mentioned above can be used across any situation in life. If you're able to master the art of listening, you can successfully defuse conflict with your coworker, your spouse, even your teenage daughter.

SARA BLAKELY, *Founder and CEO of Spanx*

Most couples fight over inconsequential things—the dishes, how you drive or park the car, who takes out the garbage. In good relationships, couples actively de-escalate conflicts by doing things like injecting well-timed humor into tense and difficult situations. Humor can lower the tension level of an argument, destroy the division between you and your partner, and remind you that you're human.

Spanx founder Sara Blakely has been married to entrepreneur Jesse Itzler for 15 years. Life can be heavy, she says, and having someone who can lighten the mood or make you laugh is one of the most important things. So when she and Itzler get in a heated argument, he extends his hand, and they slow dance. "It's really helpful," Blakely says. "We respect that each of us moves at a fast pace. That might bother some, but we get it."

DANNY MEYER,
Restaurateur

Famed restaurateur Danny Meyer once said, "Make new mistakes every day. Don't waste time repeating the old ones." In an industry that requires a certain level of consistency and perfectionism, how does he encourage his team to experiment and take risks often without the fear of failure?

He has a method he calls "The 5 As of Mistake-Making." He explains, "The first is to be aware you made the mistake. Second, acknowledge it. Third, apologize for it. Fourth, act on it and fix it. And fifth, apply additional generosity."

SHARPENING YOUR RELATIONAL SKILLSET

We got married in July 2020—during a global pandemic, a tropical storm, and a nationwide state of social unrest.

I had been a newlywed for less than a day, and already realized that there was so much I had yet to learn—and many more times I'd get blindsided by life.

So naturally, I asked the readers of my newsletter **THE PROFILE** to share their best marriage advice. Thanks to their answers, I learned one important thing: Most everything in life is a skill that can be mastered. (Yes, even the sacred, mushy, intangible thing we call "love.")

More than 100 couples weighed in with sage advice including, "Conduct regular relationships audits," "Restrain yourself from being petty," and "Give life to each other's dreams."

*Make
new mistakes
every day.
Don't waste
time repeating
the old
ones.*

**DANNY
MEYER**

But something I noticed after speaking to couples who have been married for 5, 15, or 30 years is that they never thought they were done learning how to be a better partner. In other words, they understood that a loving partnership is a constant work in progress, and there's always room for improvement.

The beauty of this mindset is that you can take action the second you finish reading this chapter. You may not be perfect, but you can improve. You may not always get it right, but you can practice until you do.

Psychologist John Gottman has spent more than 40 years studying divorce prediction and marital stability. He's researched all sorts of relationships over the decades by using applied mathematics to create what he calls "love equations."

In his most famous study, Gottman set up an apartment-like laboratory called the "Love Lab" at the University of Washington. He videotaped thousands of newlyweds, which allowed him to dissect their interactions into hard, quantifiable data.

From the data he gathered, Gottman separated the couples into two major groups: the **masters** and the **disasters**. He found that the masters were still happily together after six years, whereas the disasters had either broken up or were chronically unhappy in their marriages.

Gottman has developed models, scales, and formulas to better predict marital stability and divorce in couples. His research focuses on the process of conflict within a marriage—the way couples fight and reconcile—and less on the content of the argument.

Based on his research and experience in the last several decades, Gottman can predict with up to 94% accuracy whether couples—straight or gay, rich or poor, childless or not—will break up or live happily ever after. He co-founded the Gottman Institute with his partner and wife Julie in 1996.

The Gottmans are focused on helping the couples they

work with become skilled at navigating the obstacles that will inevitably pop up in their relationships.

"If you do nothing to make things get better in your marriage but do not do anything wrong, the marriage will still tend to get worse over time," Gottman writes in his book *Why Marriages Succeed or Fail: And How to Make Yours Last.* "To maintain a balanced emotional ecology, you need to make an effort—think about your spouse during the day, think about how to make a good thing even better, and act."

It's the *act* part of his statement that makes Gottman so effective in his work. Let's explore several strategies that he recommends that make partnerships of all kinds last.

The first is to make sure that your relationship follows **the 5-to-1 ratio.**

Here's the crazy thing about any relationship in life: It's the mundane moments that determine its health and longevity. One of his most concrete findings is that happier couples had a ratio of five positive interactions to every negative interaction. The interactions don't have to be grand gestures. "A smile, a head nod, even just grunting to show you're listening to your partner—those are all positive," Gottman says.

That's because this magic ratio enhances the positivity in your relationship. For instance, even if you're tired, you might remind yourself to do something thoughtful or nice for your partner. As long as there are more positive interactions for every negative one, you're in the green zone.

Second, Gottman says he can distinguish between the relationship masters and the relationship disasters based on whether couples answer each other's **"bids."**

He refers to "bids" as the random requests for connection partners make throughout the day. Say that your partner is a car enthusiast and notices a vintage Chevrolet Corvette on the road. He might urge you to look by saying, "Look at that car!" Even

'Small things often' is so much more important than 'big things occasionally.'

JOHN GOTTMAN

though it may sound trivial, your partner is requesting a response, or making "a bid for emotional connection." Happy couples acknowledge and respond to each other's bids even if it's just for a quick moment. Gottman believes in the motto: "'Small things often' is so much more important than 'big things occasionally.'"

Finally, Gottman says **the skill of repairment** is crucial in the formation of a long-lasting relationship. But what if you just had a big blowout fight? Is it too late?

Don't worry—even happy couples have ugly screaming matches and stonewall each other. They do many of the same things unhealthy couples do, but at some point they have a conversation where they recover from the argument.

The difference is that healthy couples have effective strategies to repair the conflict quickly rather than letting it fester. Gottman describes a repair attempt as "any statement or action—silly or otherwise—that prevents negativity from escalating out of control." It could be anything from a smile to taking a break to asking for clarity.

In other words, building skills around communication, trust, and conflict resolution are the key to a happy partnership. As one reader of **THE PROFILE** told me, love is not just an emotion. It is a skill.

"It has to be worked on; sharpened regularly," he said. "Much like any other craft, the time that goes into keeping it fresh and vibrant must be respected. And like all important skills, it must be used."

HUGH JACKMAN,
Actor

Hugh Jackman and his wife Deborra-Lee Furness have one of the longest-lasting marriages in Hollywood.

Before they got married, they made a simple but powerful choice to "always look each other in the eye at every crossroads in life."

"Those crossroads are sometimes big, sometimes they're small, sometimes you don't even realize they're crossroads until you look back," he says.

When they come to a fork in the road where they have to make a decision, they ask each other the following question: "Is this good or bad for our family?" As often as possible, they do the thing that is good for the family.

CHARLIE MUNGER,
Investor

Inspired by the German mathematician Carl Gustav Jacob Jacobi, Charlie Munger says, "Invert, always invert." Most of us attempt to solve our problems one way—forward. But Munger says there's a benefit to approaching the problem from the opposite end.

Here's how the mental model works: You flip the problem around and think backward. For example, rather than asking, "What new behaviors can I take on to ensure I have a successful marriage?" it might be more useful to ask, "What behaviors could ruin my marriage?" Avoiding the most common behaviors that lead to divorce may be more helpful than trying to figure out the ingredients for a successful partnership.

Bits of GENIUS

Trust compounds. So does mistrust.

Consistency is key. Eventually you get a seamless web of deserved trust. And life—and business—become much simpler.

Listening, mirroring, and labeling allow you to defuse even the most extreme conflicts.

Love is a skill that can be mastered, and loving relationships are always works in progress.

Absence of conflict isn't enough for a happy or successful marriage. And grand gestures aren't what define them. It's the mundane moments.

Aim for five positive interactions for every negative interaction.

Trust compounds. And there's someone we trust above all others: Ourselves. But what if we're not always worthy of trust? What if we're not a reliable narrator? How do the world's most successful people ensure they are better storytellers in their own lives—and as professionals or creatives hoping to help and influence others? We'll discover that next.

Chapter Four

TELLING BETTER STORIES

"Great stories happen to those who can tell them."

—Ira Glass, creator of *This American Life*

AFTER A SUDDEN and unexpected breakup, Lori Gottlieb ended up on the couch of her therapist Wendell.

After patiently listening to her story, Wendell told her that she reminded him of a popular cartoon of a prisoner, shaking the bars, desperately trying to get out. But, he added, on the right and the left, the bars were open. All she had to do was walk *around* those bars.

Why didn't she?

Like many of us, Gottlieb was acting as her own jailer. She believes it all came down to a story. And that it often does—stories we tell ourselves, stories we believe, stories we are reluctant to revise.

Stories, after all, are Gottlieb's job. As a psychotherapist and writer, she sees how they form the core of our lives. They give us deeper meaning. As a writer, she asks: "What does the protagonist want, and what is keeping that person from getting it?" As a therapist, she asks the same questions.

Gottlieb says, "In both the therapy room and at my writing desk, I do a lot of editing of these stories: What material is extraneous? Is the story advancing or is the protagonist going in circles? Do the plot points reveal a theme?"

As humans, we tell stories about everything from the traumas of our childhoods to our hopes for the future. Stories determine what is beautiful, who is successful, and why our problems matter.

Have you ever considered that your life has a protagonist, supporting characters, an interesting plot, obstacles, emotion, and conflict? Our lives possess all the elements necessary for a compelling story—but who is telling it, and which parts do they choose to emphasize?

A story can change depending on the narrator—and that narrator may not always be trustworthy.

The final words in the smash-hit musical *Hamilton* are: "Who lives, who dies, and who tells your story?" As people leave the theater, they are left wondering, "Who tells *my* story?"

It's an important question to answer, because if you don't learn how to tell a compelling narrative about your own life, someone else will.

TAKING CONTROL OF THE UNRELIABLE NARRATOR

You've probably experienced the literary device of the unreliable narrator in novels such as *The Girl on the Train*, *Rebecca,* and *Fight Club*. Edgar Allen Poe's *Tell-Tale Heart* even begins with the narrator attempting to convince the reader that he is sane. (Never trust a narrator who tries to convince you he's sane.)

The twist is: We are all unreliable narrators of our own lives.

We automatically shape our stories, making sure to emphasize certain pieces of information while downplaying others.

David Carr's harrowing memoir, *The Night of The Gun,* addresses the inherent unreliability of one's own memory. Carr was a drug addict for a significant period of time, so he goes on a fact-finding mission to uncover the truth about the events of his own life. He writes:

> "In the Ebbinghaus curve, or forgetting curve, 'R' stands for memory retention, 's' is the relative strength of memory and 't' is time. The power of a memory can be built through repetition, but it is the memory we are recalling when we speak, not the event.
>
> "And stories are annealed in the telling, edited by turns each time they are recalled ... People remember what they can live with more often than how they lived."

In his quest for the absolute truth, Carr discovers that there are many versions of it depending on who you ask. Hollywood producer Robert Evans once wrote: "There are three sides to every story: yours, mine, and the truth."

As storytellers, we distort, we deny, we embellish—yet we have absolute trust in our tangled beliefs. Very few of us rigorously fact-check and verify the stories we tell ourselves. And we tend to listen to the main character alone.

As a therapist, Gottlieb says she helps patients "edit" the stories they tell themselves. In many cases, using logic isn't enough. In her TED Talk, she explains how two sets of facts can be twisted, emphasized, or minimized depending on the person telling the story. "The way we narrate our lives shapes what they become," she says. "That's the danger of our stories, because they can really mess us up, but it's also their power."

In her years speaking with patients, Gottlieb noticed that

People remember what they can live with more often than how they lived.

DAVID CARR

most people's stories tend to circle around two key themes: freedom and change. Contemplating the former makes you feel helpless, trapped, imprisoned. The latter makes you feel the sharp blade of uncertainty. In order to free yourself, you need to venture into the unknown.

Try this exercise: Start with a blank page and write about a situation that's making you anxious. What have you been telling yourself? Who made you upset? What is the problem? Now, take out another piece of paper, and write about the same situation from the perspective of a different character in your life.

Gottlieb asks, "What would happen if you looked at your story and wrote it from another person's point of view? What would you see now from this wider perspective?" Sometimes, the story you've been telling yourself about your life doesn't reflect reality at all.

This exercise is powerful because it allows you to poke holes and identify your blind spots. When there's uncertainty, Gottlieb says, we try to fill in the blanks so we feel like we have more control. "Unfortunately, we don't fill in the blanks with something positive," she adds. "We tend to fill in the blanks with something terrifying."

All of this helps us tell better, more truthful stories to ourselves. And, of course, that means we can also tell better stories to others. Improving storytelling is not just about avoiding self-sabotage, but about thriving professionally and personally.

Great storytellers get results, as we'll see next.

LIN-MANUEL MIRANDA,
Playwright

Think about all the people you pass by on the way to work each day. The person working at the front desk in your apartment building. The security guard at your office. The custodian you see bright and early every morning. Do you know their names? Do you ask them questions? Or do you rush by, too busy to even acknowledge they're there?

When we look at our days, we're often the main character and everyone else just plays a supporting role.

When he broke up with his high-school sweetheart, playwright Lin-Manuel Miranda saw himself as the romantic, heartbroken boyfriend. But what about her story? "In her story, I am not the angsty, shoulder-cracking, tortured artist. I am the obstacle in the way of her *real* love story," he says.

Exercise your empathy muscle by understanding that sometimes you're the main character, and other times you play the supporting role in someone else's story.

AL PACINO,
Actor

Legendary actor Al Pacino understands that characters, like people, have layers. They have motivations, follow incentives, and oftentimes hold conflicting emotions. This allows him to bring a sense of nuance to his performances that many other actors lack.

Because no human clearly fits into the category of solely good or bad, Pacino was able to break the Hollywood cliché of the hero always being the "good guy." For example, in *The Godfather*, Pacino portrays a violent Mafia boss but his ruthlessness is born out of love, loyalty, and the desire to protect his family.

Pacino's performances are believable because he seems so natural playing the role. That's because he doesn't pretend, he *becomes*. The actor finds a sliver of himself in the characters he's about to embody, and steps into their inner world.

When inhabiting a character, Pacino says he looks for the thing that moves him on an *emotional level*. It's not just that he knows *what* his character is saying, nor even *why* his character is saying it, but *how he feels* when saying it.

FOCUSING ON CONFLICT AND INTENT

How do you tell a story that captures the spirit of a generation? That's a tall task, but there's one person who has done it time and time again.

With films like *The Trial of the Chicago 7*, *The Social Network*, and *A Few Good Men*, screenwriter Aaron Sorkin has become a master at capturing the zeitgeist, or the moral and cultural climate of a historical period.

As someone who has literally received a "Zeitgeist Award," Sorkin has bad news. Unfortunately, the "zeitgeist" isn't something you can simply choose to produce. "That's not a writable thing," he says. "The only writable things are intention and obstacle."

One of Sorkin's most popular films is *The Social Network*, the film that dramatizes the founding of Facebook. When Sorkin was writing the screenplay, two lawsuits had been brought against the company, and the plaintiffs and defendants ended up telling *three* different versions of the same story.

Sorkin didn't want to pick one version of the truth. "I liked that there were three different, and oftentimes conflicting, versions of the truth. I wanted to tell all three versions."

In other words, he masterfully used the unreliable narrator device we mentioned in the previous section to create a cocktail of chaos. And it proved incredibly compelling. Because what happens when there are three versions of the truth thanks to a multitude of unreliable narrators?

Conflict.

When telling a story, it's important to remember that **conflict** is the key ingredient of any narrative. Here's how Sorkin defines it: "Somebody wants something, and something's standing in their way of getting it. It doesn't matter what they want— they want the money, they want the girl, they want to get to Philadelphia. Doesn't matter. But they've got to want it bad. If they can *need* it, that's even better."

But there's a catch: Conflict is nothing if it isn't laced with intent.

Sorkin's hidden genius is that he never tells the audience who a character is but rather shows them what a character wants. This is important because it introduces **intent**. In other words, what lies behind the character's action? Why are they motivated to do what they do?

In *The Social Network*, Mark Zuckerberg's character is embroiled in all sorts of conflict—with his girlfriend, with his friend Eduardo, with the Winklevoss twins who claimed they invented Facebook, and of course, with the powerful institution that is Harvard.

That's the conflict, which is immediately followed by the

The only writable things are intention and obstacle.

AARON SORKIN

intent. In the film, Zuckerberg is willing to burn everything to the ground in order to prove his worth—whether it means losing a relationship, a friend, a cofounder, an investor, or a fancy finals club party invite. Ultimately, the intent is gaining social status. And he plows through every obstacle until he attains it.

"For me, this was never about Facebook," Sorkin says. "I'm not somebody who's as interested in technology as other people. What I saw was—against a very modern backdrop—a story as old as storytelling itself: [A]bout friendship, loyalty, power, betrayal, class, jealousy."

As long as you take the listener on a journey filled with conflict and intent, you've got a compelling narrative worth telling and retelling.

Here's Sorkin's **simple test for storytelling**: You don't have a story unless you can use the words "but," "except," or "and then," which means an obstacle has been introduced and now there's conflict. In other words, you need to ask yourself: **"What does this character want, and what is standing in their way of getting it?"**

So how can you use Sorkin's conflict-centric framework for your own benefit?

- If you're **an entrepreneur pitching an investor**, you could tell a story about a frustrated user who encounters a thorny problem that your product solves. For instance, Airbnb's original slide deck led with the idea that price-sensitive consumers wanted to save money when traveling, but they had no easy way to book an affordable room with a local resident.

- If you're a **salesperson**, you need to persuade your client to purchase your product. Here's a quick tip from beer entrepreneur Jim Koch: "You have a viable business if your product is either better or cheaper." So you can tell the prospective client a story that describes your competitor's product as low in quality or high in price. Your competitors create problems, while you offer a solution.

- If you're **pursuing a romantic partner**, you could outline all the obstacles standing in your way—geographical distance, for example—and offer solutions as to how to make the relationship work because your intent is to be together against all odds.

Focusing on conflict and intent makes your storytelling better because it introduces friction and tension. You don't have to tell the audience who a character is—you can show them what a character wants.

MELANIE PERKINS, *Cofounder and CEO of Canva*

When you search the words "bizarre pitch deck," Melanie Perkins's Canva recruitment pitch deck often appears as the first result. Here's why: As Perkins was building up Canva's technical team, she wanted to recruit Dave Hearnden, a senior engineer at Google, but he was reluctant to leave his role at the tech giant.

He was having second thoughts, so Perkins hatched a plan to convince him to take a chance on Canva. She sent him a very simplistic 16-slide pitch deck, which details the story of a protagonist named Dave. The conflict? He longed for adventure but was torn by his loyalty for Google. Finally, Dave was approached by a company named Canva with an exciting proposition: "Transform the world of design."

In the pitch deck, as in real life, Dave eventually joined Canva.

> **No one is inherently boring. They're only boring because you haven't asked the right questions.**
>
> **MY JOURNALISM PROFESSOR**

VINCE GILLIGAN,
Writer and showrunner

Storytelling requires motion, and the characters have to drive the narrative forward.

Vince Gilligan, creator of hit TV series *Breaking Bad*, always asks his team of writers these three questions: 1) What does the character want right now? 2) What are they afraid of? And 3) What stands between them and their goal?

FINDING THE EXTRAORDINARY IN THE MUNDANE

When I was in college, my journalism professor gave us a dream assignment: Write a profile of someone of your choosing.

Although I was excited to interview a fellow classmate, I didn't realize how challenging it would be. The person was timid and didn't readily share a life story full of surprises and intrigue. I was confused. I thought this would be easy.

So I landed in my professor's office after my interview, and I told him that I had to choose someone else because I had somehow chosen "the most boring person in the world."

My professor refused.

He recognized that I hadn't done my job as an interviewer. He told me, "No one is inherently boring. They're only boring because you haven't asked the right questions."

And that quote has carried me through my career as a reporter and storyteller. Whenever I hit a rough patch, I always remind myself that it's not the subject's duty to entertain me. As the storyteller, it's up to me to find the extraordinary in the mundane.

This realization came into full view when I interviewed Brandon Stanton, the photographer behind the popular blog *Humans of New York*.

Stanton has spent more than ten years capturing the fascinating stories of ordinary people. He catches his subjects at various moments in time—from their most vulnerable to their most philosophical. *Humans of New York* features portraits of strangers who share intimate stories of strength, addiction, redemption, regret, and love.

"First, it was just photographing who was on the street, then I started interviewing people on the street, and then I started learning stories from people on the street," he told me. "It's realizing that not only do the stories of ordinary people hold attention, they can be even more compelling and relatable than stories of public figures and celebrities."

While traditional media outlets often sensationalize the violence in certain parts of the world by telling stories in black-and-white terms, great storytellers find nuance and beauty in the ordinary.

Ira Glass began his career in public radio as a 19-year-old intern at NPR in 1978. There, he held nearly every possible job—tape-cutter, desk assistant, newscast writer, editor, producer, reporter, and substitute host.

Seventeen years after joining NPR, he pitched an idea for a show that would become *This American Life*, a weekly program featuring a single theme that's explored in several "acts." It's journalism but with novelistic techniques used to develop characters, scenes, and a plot.

Fast forward 28 years, Glass has inspired hundreds of podcasts and podcasters with the type of longform nonfiction audio format he pioneered in 1995.

Needless to say, *This American Life* has become a cultural staple, and it covers topics ranging from racial politics to immigration to college life in a way told through the voices of ordinary people. The stories, Glass says, "make it possible to imagine, if this happened to you, this is what it might feel like." Glass has discovered a formula for compelling storytelling that turns even the most seemingly "boring" subjects and makes them interesting.

The stories on *This American Life* follow a narrative journalism structure that includes two basic building blocks: 1) **a forward-moving plot** and 2) **a multitude of ideas**. The forward-moving plot, he says, is driven by an anecdote and a series of consecutive actions (X led to Y, which led to Z). This creates momentum and suspense. Then, he overlays the suspense with feelings and ideas which will help the listener make an emotional connection with the story.

Each episode is structured in a way that leads the listener to a "special moment," or a moment of reflection, to help them understand or empathize with the character's predicament on an intimate level.

For example, *This American Life* produced an episode featuring Republican Senator Jeff Flake. A woman who didn't agree with his politics told Glass that as she was listening, she kept thinking, "No! Don't make me *like* him!" She added, "I didn't want it to happen, but you humanized him."

And that's precisely what makes ordinary stories extraordinary. Glass says the point is to document a human being—with all their ideals, quirks, and flaws—and allow the listener to form an opinion about the person on their own.

Regardless of medium, the devil's always in the mundane details. My favorite example of the "it's-the-boring-that-makes-you-interesting" phenomenon is the mother of all profiles. Gay Talese's famous 1966 *Esquire* profile, "Frank Sinatra Has a

Cold," became the gold standard of profile writing even though he never once spoke with Sinatra himself. The story became one of the most celebrated magazine stories ever published. It's often considered one of history's greatest celebrity profiles. This iconic feature pioneered a form of "new journalism" that paired factual reporting with the kind of vivid storytelling that had previously been reserved for fiction.

Talese went to L.A. hoping to score an interview with Sinatra, but the legendary singer was under the weather and unwilling to be interviewed. So Talese spoke with more than 100 people in Sinatra's world and observed the legendary singer from afar. It makes for a ton of mundane moments that depict a fascinating, nuanced portrait of Sinatra in his prime.

For example:

> "Sinatra with a cold is Picasso without paint, Ferrari without fuel—only worse. For the common cold robs Sinatra of that uninsurable jewel, his voice, cutting into the core of his confidence, and it affects not only his own psyche but also seems to cause a kind of psychosomatic nasal drip within dozens of people who work for him, drink with him, love him, depend on him for their own welfare and stability. A Sinatra with a cold can, in a small way, send vibrations through the entertainment industry and beyond as surely as a President of the United States, suddenly sick, can shake the national economy."

It's a brilliant story. You are captivated immediately, and can't stop reading. Yet here's what struck me about Talese: The Sinatra piece isn't his favorite.

Rather, he points to his first profile for *Esquire* called "Mr. Bad News," a story on an obscure obituary writer no one had heard of before Talese dedicated 5,000 words to him.

One of Talese's golden rules for being a successful writer is to develop an intellectual curiosity. He has always understood the value of the stories of "all those ordinary people," and he worked to bring them to life in his early days at the *New York Times*.

"I'd wander the streets of the city to see somebody feeding pigeons," he says. "I started writing about doormen and bus drivers and all the people who blend into the city. I wanted to know, 'What were their lives like?'"

Talese says people don't have to be important in terms of fame or achievement because "everybody has a story." If you take the time to pay attention, ask questions, and listen, you'll find that the most extraordinary stories hide in the most ordinary-seeming individuals.

"When you're an obscure person yourself and you identify with obscurity, or you go through life wondering about people, it strikes within me and resonates within me so richly," he says.

Ultimately, we are all ordinary people with the power to tell extraordinary stories—all that's required is a genuine curiosity for our fellow humans. That's where the juiciest, most interesting details hide.

Stanton uses the following **three questions** when he meets a stranger: 1) "What's your biggest struggle?" 2) "How has your life turned out differently than you expected it to?" and 3) "What do you feel most guilty about?"

But it's not the questions that elicit vulnerability—it's being completely present and genuinely curious. It's what my college professor wanted me to understand: Ask great questions, and you'll get great stories.

Remember the words of Ira Glass in the opening of this chapter: "Great stories happen to those who can tell them."

FRED ROGERS,
Host of Mister Rogers' Neighborhood

The grand gestures, the fancy dinners, the awards and honors—Fred Rogers said none of these things are what "nourishes the soul."

A high-school student once asked him, "What was the greatest event in American history?" He couldn't say because it was likely something simple with little to no fanfare ("such as someone forgiving someone else for a deep hurt that eventually changed the course of history").

"The really important 'great' things are never the center stage of life's dramas; they're always 'in the wings,'" he said. "That's why it's so essential for us to be mindful of the humble and the deep rather than the flashy and the superficial."

Bits of GENIUS

Create stories about yourself, told by other characters, to find different perspectives on your problems and identify blind spots.

You're not always the main character in life. Playing a supporting role in others' stories is important too.

The secret to compelling storytelling lies in conflict. Use the words "but," "except" or "and then" to find it. Then layer intent in to make it meaningful. What motivates the people in the story you're telling?

People are only boring if you ask the wrong questions.

Create momentum and suspense by ensuring your story's plot is built of consecutive actions: X leads to Y, which leads to Z, which...

Bring the audience into a subject's dilemmas, and they'll empathize with them—even if they don't want to.

Extraordinary stories lurk in ordinary places, if you have the curiosity and patience to find them. Try asking people about their biggest struggle; how their life has turned out differently than expected; and what they feel most guilty about.

Becoming a master storyteller can have profound benefits for ourselves and others. But we're not always the narrator. Sometimes it's important to let others have the floor. That's more important than ever when it comes to being an effective leader—as the world's most successful leaders know, and as we'll see next.

Chapter Five

BECOMING A MORE EFFECTIVE LEADER

"There is someone somewhere who is looking at you and learning from you.

KYLE CARPENTER

W E OFTEN IMAGINE leaders to be those heading large corporations or taking soldiers through war, but the truth is you're a leader if you're a parent, a teacher, or an older sibling.

As Medal of Honor recipient Kyle Carpenter said, "There is someone somewhere who is looking at you and learning from you. You can be extraordinary in the most normal occasions and settings."

Although you may picture a boisterous CEO when you hear the word "leader," I've discovered that it's quite the opposite when it comes to truly great management. It may seem counterintuitive, but the best leaders are those who aim to become *invisible.*

In this chapter, we'll learn just how to do that—as well as other techniques the world's best use to become better leaders at home and at work.

INVERTING
THE PYRAMID

Many leaders think of themselves at the top of a pyramid, and as a result, employ a top-down approach at their organizations.

But what if there was a more efficient and innovative way to manage a team?

Over the last decade, Spotify founder Daniel Ek has developed a non-conventional leadership playbook at the music-streaming behemoth.

Ek, who is personally reserved but professionally ruthless, employs a fresh approach to creativity and leadership. He likes to go on long walks that help him sharpen his thinking. He looks to Beyoncé for ideas on the creative process. He refuses to schedule more than three meetings per day.

But most surprisingly, he's not a top-down leader at an organization where structure is key. Ek once heard the CEO of Scandinavian Airlines say that the right way to think about leadership is to flip the top-down model. "You should invert the pyramid and envision yourself as the guy at the bottom," Ek says. "You are there to enable all the work being done. That's my mental image of what I'm here to do at Spotify."

In a bottom-up management approach, the ideas, values, and strategies come mostly from the employees who are the lifeblood of the company, while the C-suite executives offer support and resources to help the team execute plans quickly.

For example, Ek was originally against a product team's idea to roll out Discover Weekly, a personalized Spotify playlist that updates weekly for each user. He questioned them multiple times and asked why they were spending all that time and energy working on the feature. "I would have killed that if it was just me, 100%," he told *Fast Company* in 2018. "I never really saw the beauty of it."

The team continued working on it despite Ek's lack of enthusiasm. And then suddenly, they launched it to the public. "I remember reading about it in the press," Ek said. "I thought, Oh, this is going to be a disaster."

Discover Weekly became one of Spotify's most loved product features.

Ek says his role in the inverted pyramid structure is to

empower internal leaders and direct the necessary resources so they can execute their ideas. "I'll provide people a rough direction," he explains. "I won't provide them all of the things that they need in order to get there."

This grassroots-type leadership approach is difficult to implement because employees typically look to the CEO for answers and guidance—especially in times of crisis. But the hidden genius of the greatest leaders is that they understand flipping the pyramid has the power to generate better ideas even in the most chaotic times.

Famed restaurateur Danny Meyer has weathered multiple crises as a leader, including the 9/11 attacks, the 2008 financial crisis, and most recently, a global pandemic. Like Ek, he sees himself as "a bottom-up manager who subscribes to the concept of 'servant leadership.'"

Servant leadership was popularized by the late Robert Greenleaf, who believed that organizations are at their most effective when leaders encourage collaboration, trust, foresight, listening, and empowerment. "In any hierarchy, it's clear that the ultimate boss (in my case, me) holds the most power," Meyer writes in his memoir, *Setting the Table*. "But a wonderful thing happens when you flip the traditional organizational chart upside down so that it looks like a V with the boss on the bottom."

That wonderful thing? Fresh ideas. Research has found that "servant leaders" create a climate of trust, which motivates employees to take risks and push the company forward.

The Covid-19 pandemic forced Meyer's company, Union Square Hospitality Group, to shutter 19 restaurants, its events business, and lay off 2,000 people. During that time, he received an email from one of his team members. She was pregnant and told him that her due date was supposed to be the happiest day of her life. Instead, it coincided with the end of her ability to pay her healthcare premiums.

Meyer had a brainstorming session with his team, and they presented an idea: Instead of creating GoFundMe campaigns for fellow employees who had been affected by a crisis, why not create an employee relief fund for Union Square Group members?

As the CEO, Meyer signed off on it, and contributed 100% of his salary and all gift card sales to it. In total, it raised $1.5 million, which went to former employees.

Experimentation is often the first thing to freeze during a crisis, but Meyer believes it's the difference between life and death for a business. He often tells his staff, "Make new mistakes every day. Don't waste time repeating the old ones."

When I asked him about his mistake-making philosophy in an industry that requires a certain level of consistency and perfectionism, he told me it was simple: "If you have a culture of fear where people are afraid of getting in trouble because they made an honest mistake, you're going to have a much lower rate of innovation."

By flipping the pyramid, Meyer is able to foster growth, authority, and leadership in the very people who are the lifeblood of the restaurant. He writes, "A balanced combination of uncompromising standards and confidence-building reassurance sends a very clear and consistent message to your team: 'I believe in you and I want you to win as much as I want to win.'"

LEYMAH GBOWEE,
Nobel Peace Laureate

Leymah Gbowee is an activist who helped end a 14-year civil war in Liberia by uniting women in a movement that advocated for peace.

During a Q&A, a Nigeria-born Columbia University student asked Gbowee how Africans educated in the West could create meaningful change in their native countries if they were to return. "Please do not adopt a mentality that 'We are going back to save them,'" Gbowee said. "Look at me. Even with your Columbia education, can you save me? Honestly? Child, don't try it when you go to Nigeria."

It takes time to earn trust, build credibility, and truly understand the needs of the people who live there every day. "Go with an attitude of wanting to learn, wanting to serve, and not that 'I've lived in New York and I come back with a Columbia education.' Or you will come running back to the U.S."

True leadership, according to Gbowee, is empowering others rather than hoarding the power yourself.

ESTHER WOJCICKI,
Educator

Struggling to implement rules in your household? Educator Esther Wojcicki recommends trying a bottom-up approach within your own family.

For instance, if you want to limit the time your kids spend in front of a screen, call a family meeting and tell them you want *them* to come up with fair rules.

Allow your kids to be part of the rule-making process, and you might be pleasantly surprised with what they come up with. The more you involve your children in a democratic process where their ideas are listened to, challenged, and respected, the more they'll learn to do the same for others.

ROBERT CIALDINI,
Social psychologist

As a leader, you want input from your team so you can cultivate a democratic culture within your company. How? You need to create a sense of unity, collaboration, and togetherness.

Robert Cialdini, a social psychologist who has been called "the godfather of influence," says you can do this by changing one word in your vocabulary. Rather than asking people for their opinion, ask them for their *advice*. "It invites partnership," he says. "The idea of advice is associated with collaboration and togetherness."

SYSTEMATIZING YOUR LIFE

Shopify founder and CEO Tobi Lütke is obsessed with using systems to solve problems in business and in life.

He has a simple rule about efficiency: "If I have to do something once, that's fine. If I have to do it twice, I'm kind of annoyed. And if I have to do it three times, I'm going to try to automate it."

The biggest advantage Lütke says he's had as an entrepreneur is that he started out as a programmer, because programming taught him to think in systems. "By default, most people think about cause and effect, but the world doesn't work like that. The world actually works in systems—it is loopy, not linear," he says.

A company, like life, is made up of multiple complex systems

If I have to do something once, that's fine. If I have to do it twice, I'm kind of annoyed. And if I have to do it three times, I'm going to try to automate it.

TOBI LÜTKE

that influence one another. Things are rarely cut and dried. There are systems around everything from organization to communication to incentives.

Lütke believes that if you want to start getting better results you need to focus on the system, not the outcome. But what does that look like in practice?

First, let's note the difference between an outcome-based mindset and a systems-based mindset.

Say you make a mistake. An **outcome-based mindset** would prevent you from making that one, specific mistake again—while **a systems-based mindset** would prevent you from making that specific mistake along with hundreds of future similar mistakes because you've figured out the root cause of *why* you made the mistake in the first place.

Lütke offers this great piece of advice: "Always understand the system of how you got to where you are."

Entrepreneurship, he says, is about the ability to step back and look at the whole picture. "It's a beautiful thing as an early company—if you have ten people, and one product, and one potential market, you can actually draw the entire systems diagram on one blackboard," he says. "Once you have that modeled out, try to reason about the whole situation and pick out how you got to the point. That's what the trick is."

For instance, Lütke uses a color-coding technique to manage his calendar. He labels anything product-related as red, investor and board of directors-related business as teal, and so on. The thing he's looking for is a balanced week—"A week where, ideally, I manage to devote about 30% of the time—at least—to the product and then as much as possible to things like recruiting, bigger picture projects, and one-on-ones." Color-coding your calendar is a micro-system that helps you conduct an audit to see exactly where you're spending most of your time.

Systems also act like a map that can guide you out of moments of adversity. In a systems-based organization, information flows freely and there's a clear blueprint for problem-solving.

Melanie Perkins, the CEO of design platform Canva, says systems became critical as the company matured. When it was just Perkins and her cofounder Cliff Obrecht, communication was easy. "At the start, there were just a few of us sitting around one table and everyone always knew what everyone else was working on," Perkins says.

But now, Canva's employee base has ballooned to more than 2,000, making that impossible. So Perkins and her leadership team devised a systems-based plan to make sure communication is seamless across teams.

Throughout the week, each team catches up on the daily progress toward benchmarks they want to hit. On Fridays, each team at Canva convenes for a company-wide stand-up meeting to share progress, lessons, and takeaways. "Our structure of small, empowered teams enables everyone to be nimble and move quickly," she says. This is how Canva has retained the flexibility of a start-up even though it's grown to the size of a mature corporation.

Now, let's apply systems-based thinking to your own life. In what situations could you adopt a systems-based mindset? The key is to start with the goal (or outcome) and work backwards:

- If the outcome is to **run a marathon**, the system is to create a training schedule, run a certain number of miles every day, and prepare healthy meals.
- If the outcome is to **write a book**, the system is to find a worthy topic, pitch a publisher, make an outline, and write a chapter per week.
- If the outcome is to **start a business**, the system is to identify a problem you can solve, form a team, create an operating plan, and test your product in the market.

Systems-based thinking forces you to get off autopilot, investigate the processes that run your life, and set your sights on the actions within your control.

SARA BLAKELY,
Founder of Spanx

Time is your greatest resource as an entrepreneur. As her business grew, Spanx founder Sara Blakely found herself scatterbrained and fielding questions from various departments all day long.

So she created a system she calls "bucketing your time." Rather than glossing over problems, she would dedicate entire days to focus on various tasks. For Blakely, this means Wednesdays are for creativity and branding, and Thursdays are for product ideas. "It allowed me to have context in my decision-making," she says.

MARC LORE,
Serial entrepreneur (founder of Jet.com, Diapers.com)

Most start-up culture philosophies are just that— philosophies stuck in the theoretical. When he built Jet, serial entrepreneur Marc Lore operated the company on three practical principles: "transparency, trust, and fairness."

So what did that mean in practice?

1) Transparency meant that the company was open with its information. When there was a board meeting, Lore would distribute the entire board presentation to all the

employees. He was also open about shares outstanding, share value, the difference between preferred and common stock, where employees ranked as common shareholders, and what their stock was worth.

2) Trust meant "hiring [employees] for a job, trusting that they know their job better than you and not micromanaging, and giving them the rope and the resources to do their job."

3) Fairness meant that Jet had a compensation system where everyone at the same level got the exact same pay.

BOB BOWMAN,
Long-time coach of Olympic legend Michael Phelps

Bob Bowman says you need a system of tiny short-term goals that are achievable. For example, if your goal is to go to the Olympics, you need to figure out what you need to do in the next year. That means breaking it down into very specific events, including the exact times you want to get.

The basis of Bowman's program is that the process of success is more important than any outcome. In other words, if you focus on the process, the results will take care of themselves. Bowman often quotes legendary college football coach Nick Saban: "Don't look at the scoreboard; play the next play."

The thoughts you think, Bowman emphasizes, affect how you perform. "I tell them, 'Gold medals are out of your control. Another swimmer may simply be better than you on race day,'" Bowman writes in his book *Golden Rules*. "But if they set their sights on breaking a record—at nailing the best time possible—then they can visualize something that's tangible, achievable, and within their control."

Don't look at the scoreboard; play the next play.

NICK SABAN

THE POWER OF INVISIBLE LEADERSHIP

Mark Bertolini doesn't match the image you have of a buttoned-up, clean-cut Fortune 500 CEO.

Known for sporting tattoos, leather jackets, and a large skull ring, Bridgewater Associates co-CEO Bertolini is a self-described "radical capitalist."

Radical capitalism refers to the actions he took in the workplace before it was cool to do so. He raised the minimum wage, waived out-of-pocket costs, paid back student loans, and invested further in the development of his employees.

But Bertolini wasn't always this empathetic, enlightened figure. Growing up in a blue-collar family in Detroit, he was determined to succeed. He graduated with a degree in accounting from Wayne State University (although it took him eight years because he flunked out twice), and then went on to get his MBA from Cornell.

In his early career, Bertolini was unapologetically competitive, aggressive, and at times ruthless. He was so well known for his bare-knuckled, iron-fist leadership that his employees gave him the moniker Darth Vader.

"People used to hum the Darth Vader tune when I walked through the building because I was exacting," he told me in an interview.

By all measures, he had made it. He was making tons of money, living in a mansion, and earning respect in his field. But it came at a cost. He was spending more and more time away from his family, and inadvertently creating a work culture that didn't reflect his values.

And then he had two life-altering wake-up calls. In 2001, his son Eric was diagnosed with a rare and deadly form of lymphoma, and then in 2004, Bertolini broke his neck in five places in a skiing accident.

He said the two experiences made him realize the U.S. healthcare system isn't equipped to help patients recover properly after facing a major health issue. He began to define "health" broadly—a healthy individual is a productive individual, who in turn is a happy individual.

As the CEO of healthcare benefits company Aetna at the time, Bertolini began making changes from within. While the company was thriving, its employees were not, with many of them using Medicaid and food stamps. He revamped employee benefits, including a minimum wage increase to $16 an hour, and implemented yoga and meditation classes.

He realized that the employees of a company are not merely "a tool of capitalism." He learned that they are the cornerstone of any organization, and without an engaged employee base a company is bound to fail.

Exceptional leaders, Bertolini believes, do two things: 1) They understand their employees' needs and 2) They get the hell out of the way.

He learned the first lesson from his father. When Bertolini was 14 years old, he worked at his dad's auto shop making $1.25 an hour. One day, he found out that his coworker Jerry, who was in his 20s, was making $4.25 an hour.

Bertolini confronted his dad, leading to the following exchange:

"Dad, I'm making a buck and a quarter, Jerry's making four and a quarter. I want a raise."

"If I don't give you a raise, what are you going to do?"

"I'll quit."

"Really? You're going to quit? Do you have another job?"

"No."

"Great, then you're fired, stupid. Go home."

Afterward, his dad used the incident as a teaching moment. He asked Bertolini if he knew Jerry's story and then told him, "Jerry's a great guy. He's got a family. He's paying rent. He's got a young child. And Jerry's about at the pinnacle of what he's going to do for the rest of his life. And so I'm helping support Jerry's family. That's why I'm paying $4.25 an hour."

He asked Bertolini if he wanted his job back, and after he enthusiastically said yes, his dad said: "Great, you're at a buck an hour," cutting his salary by 25 cents.

This experience taught Bertolini the value of earning a living, why entitlement will never get you anywhere, and how a true leader is intimately aware of his employees' needs.

Bertolini learned the second leadership lesson after he began studying Eastern religions. He was inspired by a passage from the foundational Taoist text, the *Tao Te Ching*, attributed to philosopher Lao Tzu.

Bertolini thought about how he could apply it to business leadership. He came up with **"The Four Levels of Taoist Leadership."**

Here's how he described it to *Business Insider* in 2019: "The first level is your employees hate you. The second level is your employees fear you. The third level is your employees praise you. The fourth level, you're invisible because your organization takes care of itself."

This is the *Tao Te Ching* passage that inspired Bertolini's leadership philosophy:

"When the Master governs, the people
are hardly aware that he exists.

"Next best is a leader who is loved.

Next, one who is feared.
The worst is one who is despised.

"If you don't trust the people,
you make them untrustworthy.

"The Master doesn't talk, he acts.
When his work is done,
the people say, 'Amazing:
we did it, all by ourselves!'"

Bertolini's final chapter at Aetna involved shepherding the sale of Aetna to CVS Health. As a leader, your legacy should be to arm your people with the skills to propel your organization into the future—without you.

BERNARD ARNAULT, CEO of LVMH (Louis Vuitton Moët Hennessy)

With a roster of more than 70 brands including Fendi, Bulgari, Dom Pérignon, and Givenchy, Bernard Arnault has built the world's largest and most successful purveyor of luxury goods.

Many people see Arnault as a great financier, CEO, and strategic businessman, but few understand that his most important role as a leader is to be a *creativity enabler.*

Throughout his career, Arnault says, he has always trusted the creatives at each fashion house. "If you think and act like a typical manager around creative people—with rules, policies, data on customer preferences, and so forth—you will quickly kill their talent," he says. "When a creative team believes in a product, you have to trust the team's gut instinct."

> *If you think and act like a typical manager around creative people ... you will quickly kill their talent.*
>
> **BERNARD ARNAULT**

You can have the best CEO, great marketing, and a brilliant business strategy, but without a driving creative force, you have nothing. When you're in the business of innovation and originality, Arnault says your first and foremost priority as a leader should be the quality of the product. Know when to step aside and trust your team.

BRUNELLO CUCINELLI,
Fashion mogul

Fashion mogul Brunello Cucinelli understands that investing in your people is a strategy that pays off in the long run. He pays his employees a higher wage than the market rate. The whole company takes a 90-minute lunch break; employees can go home to feed their families or eat at the heavily subsidized company cafeteria.

He has also installed a library where workers and visitors are encouraged to peruse works by Dante, Kafka, Proust, Ruskin, Rawls, Nietzsche, Derrida, and Deleuze, in many different languages.

Here's his thought process: "If I give you the right conditions to work, and I put you in a beautiful place, where you feel a little bit better about yourself because you know your work is being used for something greater than producing a profit, maybe you will get more creative."

Bits of GENIUS

The most effective leaders flip the pyramid—and lead from the bottom up, not top-down.

With servant leadership, ideas, values, and strategies come from employees—while execs offer support and resources so teams can execute their plans. This can work in organizations of every size—even in families.

Focus on perfecting systems instead of outcomes, and the outcomes take care of themselves.

Systems-based thinking forces you to get out of autopilot, investigate the processes that run your life, and set your sights on actions within your control.

Exceptional leaders understand their employees' needs—then get the hell out of the way.

Providing support and perfecting processes as a leader is all well and good—but what about making the big decisions that no one else can make? What about the defining calls in your personal life? The world's most successful people have tried-and-tested methods for that too, as we're about to find out.

Chapter Six

TAKING RISKS IN TIMES OF UNCERTAINTY

GARRETT MCNAMARA DOESN'T surf waves. He surfs sea monsters. The professional big wave surfer is the former Guinness World Record holder for the largest wave ever surfed, a 78-foot wall of water.

What does it feel like to surf a wave that size?

"The best thing I can compare riding one of these waves to is making the conscious decision to be chased down by a moving avalanche, staying as close to it as possible, actually hoping to be engulfed by it, and then somehow escaping," McNamara says.

McNamara is religious about his preparation process. Before he goes out to surf, he does intense breathing exercises to oxygenate his body in case he gets wiped out and has to spend a significant amount of time underwater.

"First, you prepare for success and your task at hand, but you have to be a *risk technician*, evaluate all the things that could go wrong, and figure out solutions," he says.

Uncertainty is constantly lurking in our everyday lives—even in areas we don't think present any risk. But if we approach our lives as "risk technicians," evaluating our choices and aiming to mitigate uncertainty, we'll become better decision-makers overall.

What can we learn from the world's most skilled risk mitigators about navigating the chaos and uncertainty present in our own lives?

BUILDING COMPETENCE

During a regular dive in the sea, Alexey Molchanov can go 131 meters deep (about 43 stories) while holding a single breath for nearly five minutes.

In that period, his body experiences more gravitational stress than an astronaut during a launch into space. Molchanov is considered the best freediver on the planet. He often overrides his body's automatic impulses (to take a breath) and pushes past limits no other human can reach without blacking out or worse.

"I enjoy finding new boundaries and pushing them further because I know I can," he says. "I trust my skills, I trust my body, I trust my abilities, and I trust the environment. That's the combination that allows me to break the records."

And the records are many. Overall, he has set 24 world records and has earned more than 25 combined gold, silver, and bronze individual and team medals at world championship events.

To Molchanov, freediving feels "very much like flying," and it's a sport that requires equal part mastery of the mind *and* the body. "I love freediving for its constant self-improvement process where you learn how to relax or learn how to handle your fears," says Molchanov, who trains all year round. "My preparation never stops."

Practice, Molchanov believes, is the source of all preparation—in sport and in life. Practice is the precursor to competence. Once you become competent, the confidence will come on its own.

So how exactly can you become a master at, say, relaxing under extreme stress? While that sounds contradictory,

Molchanov says relaxation is a skill that can be learned through endless practice.

He has a simplified three-part process on building competence before a stressful event—whether it's preparing for a dive or an important presentation at work.

First, breathing is an indicator that tells us whether we are calm or stressed. He recommends **observing your breathing pattern**, which will tell you if you have smooth, deep breathing or shallow, panicked breathing.

Second, he says our anxiety elevates when we see a problem as a life-or-death situation that needs to be solved. Instead, Molchanov recommends **shifting your perspective** to see it as a challenge that you will enjoy overcoming rather than a situation you must suffer through. "Try to feel pleasure through the process," he says.

Third, **focus on one task at a time.** Rather than seeing a problem as a big complex tangle of varying tasks, Molchanov says you can calm yourself by asking, "What is one single task I can focus on accomplishing in this next moment?"

Competence and calm are built one breath at a time—and not just in freediving.

Astronaut Chris Hadfield went temporarily blind during a spacewalk while only holding on to the orbiting International Space Station (ISS) with one arm.

Hadfield felt his left eye slam shut in pain, but he couldn't figure out why. He obviously couldn't rub it, because he couldn't reach inside his helmet. The irritant turned out to be a drop of an oil and soap mixture, which the astronauts use to de-fog their visors.

His eye began tearing, but without gravity the tears just became a big ball of heavy moisture stuck to his eye. The ball became so big that it spilled over into his other eye, making him completely blind outside of the spaceship.

Rather than panic, Hadfield's rational mind took over and gave him options—he could call Houston, he could get his fellow astronaut Scott Parazynski to do an incapacitated crew rescue, or he could cry for a while to let the tears dilute out the gunk in his eye.

He eventually opened a vent on the side of his helmet to let some oxygen out to clear and evaporate the mixture from his eyes. And then, he continued working.

This was only possible because of one lesson he learned in astronaut training: Prepare for the worst through make-believe scenarios. Think of it as **a dress rehearsal for catastrophe**.

"While play-acting grim scenarios day in and day out may sound like a good recipe for clinical depression, it's actually weirdly uplifting," Hadfield says.

Thanks to his elaborate contingency plans and problem-solving skills, Hadfield has had a colorful career. He has successfully broken into a space station with a Swiss army knife, disposed of a live snake while piloting a plane, and figured out how to fix an ammonia leak on the ISS.

"It takes a boldness of execution and an ability to overcome fear," Hadfield says. "Fear is just a symptom of lack of preparation. The best antidote for fear is competence."

For instance, when you first learned how to ride a bicycle, you were fearful because you could crash and hurt yourself. Then, as you got better and more confident in your skills, it became silly to be afraid of a bike. Yet the bike itself didn't change—it remained just as dangerous as it always was. *You* are the one who changed. Competence breeds confidence.

"Things aren't scary," Hadfield says. "People get scared."

Hadfield says the ultimate antidote to fear of anything is altering your level of competence. Remember, he says, "competence means keeping your head in a crisis, sticking with a task even when it seems hopeless, and improvising good solutions to tough problems when every second counts."

While play-acting grim scenarios day in and day out may sound like a good recipe for clinical depression, it's actually weirdly uplifting.

CHRIS HADFIELD

LEWIS HAMILTON,
Formula 1 champion

Lewis Hamilton didn't buy his way in to Formula 1. He earned it. Unlike many of his peers, Hamilton came from humble beginnings and his racing career started with remote-control cars. He was only six years old when he won his first two trophies for remote-control car racing.

Remote-control car racing led to go-karting, which put him on a path to Formula 1. He was fast, he was talented, and he was a winner. Hamilton joined the McLaren young driver program as a 13-year-old, and he eventually got officially sponsored by the F1 team at age 22. After six years with McLaren, Hamilton joined Mercedes in 2013.

To this day, Hamilton is the first—and only—Black driver in his sport. "My dad and I would watch people like Tiger [Woods] who kind of broke the mold, and we watched in admiration. The Williams sisters also did the same," he told *The Wall Street Journal*. "We're like, 'Oh, if we could do something like that, that's going to help change the industry moving forward.'"

Like Tiger Woods and the Williams sisters, Hamilton's career was encouraged by a dominant and obsessive father figure. At go-kart races, his dad Anthony would study the fastest kid on the track and coach Hamilton on the exact point where he should brake. Hamilton became known for his aggressive driving style and braking much later (and harder) than any of the other competitors.

Hamilton built competence because he doesn't see himself as a driver racing a car, but rather as an artist honing his craft. He calls it, "building his masterpiece." Here's his framework for developing competence:

"It takes a long time to master a craft, and whilst I feel like I am mastering it, there's still more to master," he said. "There's still more to add to it. There's still more pieces to the puzzle to add. There's going to be more ups and downs along the way, but I feel like I've got the best tools now, to this point at least, to be able to deal with those."

The masterpiece attitude implies there's always more work to do, more kinks to iron out, and more lessons to learn.

NIMS PURJA, *Mountaineer*

Nims Purja is a mountaineer who has summited all 14 "death zone" peaks in the world. The fastest anyone had summited all 14 had been eight years. He did it in six months and six days.

But if there's one lesson Purja has learned from his expeditions, it's this: "Nothing goes as planned in the mountains."

On one expedition, he approached a climber who was running out of oxygen at 8,450 meters. He gave him some of his own oxygen and began helping him down the mountain.

"Conducting a rescue from 8,450 meters without oxygen when you are not acclimatized is a suicidal mission, but we knew what our bodies were capable of," he says.

So how can you be prepared for the things that are impossible to prepare for? Years of training can prepare you for that single moment that matters. Before undertaking such a mammoth endeavor, you need a certain level of self-awareness of your physical and mental capabilites.

"I think the biggest thing is about discovering your body, your limitations, and what you can do and what you can't do," he says. "That's when you have the baseline and you operate from there. For me, as I said, I didn't climb mountains since I was a kid, I was only into this field for like four or five years at that point and I'm still discovering more stuff about my body. That's what I was investing in."

CALCULATING RISK

Ukraine. Afghanistan. Iraq. Darfur. Libya. Syria. Lebanon. South Sudan. Somalia. Congo.

Over the past 20 years, war photographer Lynsey Addario has covered every major conflict and humanitarian crisis on the planet, capturing destruction and pain through the lens of her camera.

She's had a number of close calls—kidnapped in Libya, abducted in Iraq, injured in a car accident in Pakistan. But the one consistent thread throughout Addario's career is that she never puts the camera down—even in the face of extreme danger.

Perhaps the most critical part of her job is to learn how to adequately assess risk. Because if you miscalculate risk—especially in Addario's line of work—the consequences can be lethal.

On a daily (and sometimes hourly) basis, Addario has to weigh the level of danger with the importance of the story she's trying to tell. She's learned over the years that miscalculating risk can be life or death.

Addario and three of her colleagues were covering the Lybian uprising in 2011, which began as a revolution and turned into a war. The group of journalists drove into the city of Ajdabiya looking for the front line as civilians fled and Qaddafi's troops closed in. Although their driver Mohammed warned them about the gravity of the situation and urged them to retreat, they didn't listen.

The car was stopped at a military checkpoint, and Addario and her colleagues were blindfolded and kidnapped while their driver likely died as a result of the decision they made not to leave the city in time.

"We never saw Mohammed again," Addario told me. "We're assuming he was killed at that checkpoint—either executed or in crossfire. His death is on us, you know? That was completely our miscalculation."

There's a difference between **calculated risk-taking and reckless risk-taking**. The former relies on making good decisions with limited information while the latter throws caution to the wind for no good reason.

Is there a practical framework we can employ to discern between the two?

Boston Beer Company cofounder Jim Koch has been called "the Steve Jobs of Beer," and "one of the most cannily successful entrepreneurs of our time."

In 1984, Koch took a big risk—he left his cushy $250,000-a-year consulting job at Boston Consulting Group to start his own brewery using his great-great-grandfather's recipe that he found in the family's attic.

When Koch felt suffocated by his boring corporate job at BCG, he had a choice: Does he stay in his safe role at BCG or does he start a beer company with no money or experience? He was terrified at the prospect of making the wrong decision.

So he began thinking about two words: **"scary"** and **"dangerous."** Leaving BCG would be the scariest decision of his life, but staying would be dangerous because he wasn't happy and he would live a life of regrets. There are plenty of

Make reversible decisions quickly and irreversible ones deliberately.

TONI SCHNEIDER

things in life that are scary but not dangerous and vice versa. He took the risk, left his job, and founded Samuel Adams beer.

Looking at your life through this mental framework can help you make some big decisions and take a calculated risk instead of an impulsive one.

But here's the hidden genius of the world's most competent risk-takers: They understand that even if they adequately assess risk and make all the right moves, success is anything but guaranteed.

MATT MULLENWEG,
CEO of Automattic

The best advice Matt Mullenweg has ever received was about decision-making.

Toni Schneider, the former CEO of Automattic (the company behind WordPress), once told him, "Make reversible decisions quickly and irreversible ones deliberately."

This mental model is quite useful during times of uncertainty. If the decision is reversible, you can make it quickly without a ton of prior information—and you'll probably learn a lot more by making it. If the decision is irreversible, however, you should be slow, deliberate, and analytical before making it.

So ask yourself: "Is the decision I'm about to make reversible or irreversible?"

NICK SABAN,
Alabama head football coach

Before every game, Nick Saban and his other coaches have what they call a "what-if meeting." In it, they ask each other, "What if this happens? What if that happens?"

They go through hypothetical scenarios in order to be best prepared for the big day—from how many helmet snaps the equipment manager wears on his belt in case a player's helmet pops off, to a breakdown of which official is more likely to throw a pass interference flag.

There is an emergency plan for nearly every scenario because Saban is known for his rigorous process, and "never allows human nature to take over a team." In other words, he mitigates risk by leaving little room for chance.

In 2015, then-defensive coordinator Kirby Smart said, "Ninety per cent of what we talk about never comes up, but 10% of it does. When it does, you're ready and you make a good decision based on the preparation."

ACCEPTING THE DARK SIDE OF RISK

The top search entry in Google for Conrad Anker's name is: "How did Conrad Anker die?"

But after delving into his life story, I kept asking myself the opposite question: "How on earth did he *live*?"

To be clear, Anker is very much alive and well, but the mountaineering legend has had his fair share of close calls.

In 1999, Anker went on an Everest expedition and located the remains of George Mallory, the legendary British climber who perished in a 1924 attempt to reach the peak. "Everest is basically hiking up a ski slope," Anker says. "But with a 2,000-pound elephant on your chest and head."

Three months later, Anker attempted to scale the world's

14th-highest peak, Shishapangma, with fellow climbers Alex Lowe and David Bridges. Lowe was the first to notice that an accumulation of snow had started to move. Within seconds, they realized they were in the path of a massive avalanche. By the time the wall of snow reached the trio, it had accelerated to over 100 miles an hour and had spread across 500 feet of the slope. They had no other option but to run. Anker ran to the left, while Lowe and Bridges went to the right. Anker suffered broken ribs, head lacerations, and a dislocated shoulder, but he survived. Lowe and Bridges were never seen again until their bodies were found in 2016.

In a 2017 commencement speech, Anker told new graduates that life is about moments—the moment you were born, the moment you took your first step, the moment that you climbed for the first time. "Those moments are all unique," he says. "They comprise the milestones of life. The one milestone that we cannot escape is death."

There's a reason I've chosen to tell the stories of McNamara, Molchanov, Hadfield, Addario, and Anker in this chapter. They're all people with extreme professions—one misstep could cost them their life.

But their stories also illustrate the bright side to taking risks: Most situations in life aren't life or death. Most situations are survivable. This means that risk is contextual, and the level of urgency changes with perspective.

In 2015, Sheryl Sandberg was working as the Chief Operating Officer at Facebook when she and her husband David Goldberg went on a beach vacation in Mexico. While exercising in the resort's gym, Goldberg collapsed and died of severe head trauma.

After his death, Sandberg texted Facebook CEO Mark Zuckerberg saying, "Urgent, Please call."

When he read her message, Zuckerberg thought it was a work issue even though she was on vacation. Reflecting on it later, he said, "A lot of things used to be 'Urgent, please call.' These days they're not."

In a blog post titled, "The Three Sides of Risk," author and investor Morgan Housel posits that there are **three distinct aspects to risk-taking:** 1) The odds you will get hit; 2) The average consequences of getting hit; and 3) The tail-end consequences of getting hit.

It's the tail-end consequences of risk that matter in the long run, which he calls "the low-probability, high-impact events." They are the hardest to control but the ones that matter most.

When Anker and his friends attempted to scale Shishapangma, they knew they were competent climbers. They had calculated the risk of climbing to the best of their abilities. But in their case, "the low-probability, high-impact event" was the avalanche they hadn't foreseen. It came down to a simple, dumb-luck decision: Anker went to the left while they went to the right.

The point is this: When we think we have become masters of chaos, life has a way of humbling even the most competent risk-mitigators. And if we survive, there are an endless number of lessons we can learn from the experience.

As big wave surfer Garrett McNamara puts it, "I think you're a master when you realize you know nothing."

STACY MADISON,
Creator of Stacy's Pita Chips

When there's uncertainty in the world, most people tend to freeze. But the best companies and most resilient entrepreneurs are born during times of crisis.

In the 1990s, Madison was working at a restaurant and helping management open a second location. She thought her career in the restaurant industry was taking off when she

"If your experiment works perfectly, then you've learned nothing.

FRANKLIN CHANG DÍAZ'S COLLEGE PROFESSOR

was abruptly fired. Devastated, she had a lightbulb moment: "Ultimately, I circled back and thought, 'If I can work this hard for someone else, then why can't I do it for myself?'"

She took a risk and invested $5,000 into a food cart that then became a pita chip empire she sold to PepsiCo for $250 million.

At some point in our lives, we all ask ourselves the question, "What am I going to do now?" Maybe you've just graduated from college or gotten fired from your job, but that moment of reflection comes for us all.

The lesson? Move when other people aren't willing to. "Sh*t happens that you can't control—fires, accidents—that's the inflection point, the opportunity when you have to take responsibility and lead," she says.

FRANKLIN CHANG DÍAZ,
Astronaut

Franklin Chang Díaz spent 25 years at NASA, where he completed seven space shuttle missions and tied the record for most space flights, logging more than 1,600 hours in space, including three spacewalks that totaled 19 hours and 31 minutes.

When he was in college, one of his professors told him, "If your experiment works perfectly, then you've learned nothing."

At the time, he didn't understand the logic, but through the years, Chang Díaz grew to grasp it: To succeed, you have to first learn to fail.

In science, like in life, progress only comes after you've exhausted all the various paths that *didn't* work in order to get to the one that does. "Take small risks frequently rather than huge risks seldom," he says. "My philosophy has always been to take small steps and lots of them."

Bits of GENIUS

Risk is everywhere, but it doesn't have to defeat us. Adopting the approach of a risk technician—evaluating and mitigating risk dispassionately—can help us make effective decisions.

Relax under stress by slowing your breathing; re-conceiving of stress as a challenge to enjoy overcoming; and focusing on one task at a time. Competence and calm are built one breath at a time.

Prepare for the worst through make-believe scenarios— dress rehearsals for catastrophe.

For every action that feels scary, there's a danger to not acting too. Remembering that can help you break a deadlock and make a rational decision.

Not every scenario requires the same amount of thought.

Reduce your decision-making burden by making reversible decisions quickly, and irreversible decisions slowly.

Tail-end risks are the hardest to control but the ones that matter most. Most risks simply aren't life or death.

Take lots of small risks regularly rather than huge ones rarely. It's a more antifragile way to make progress.

Getting comfortable with risk and making effective decisions is nothing, of course, without vision that can be trusted. How do outperformers clarify their thinking? Let's explore.

Chapter Seven

CLARIFYING YOUR THINKING

DO YOU *really* believe what you believe? What would it take to change your mind?

In 2019, I interviewed Blackstone CEO Steve Schwarzman, a man who has been called "the master of the alternative universe" because Blackstone made its name by investing in alternative assets—investments that were once considered "nontraditional," like hedge funds, private equity, and commodities.

But there's an alternative to the alternatives. Today, a new cohort of investors is plowing cash into digital assets such as Bitcoin and other cryptocurrencies.

When I asked Schwarzman what he thinks about Bitcoin, he said, "I don't have much interest in it because it's hard for me to understand. I was raised in a world where someone needs to control currencies."

Fair point. But his answer made me think about all the things we believe because of our background, our family, our job, our economic incentives, and our political affiliations. And it's only natural that our beliefs evolve over time, right?

Well, not really. In today's society, changing your mind isn't as celebrated as you might assume. In politics, you're called a flip-flopper. In real life, you're a hypocrite. On Twitter, you're god knows what.

So we stick to our beliefs—no matter how wrong or outdated—and forge ahead. Why? Because we're searching for social acceptance and identity validation, much more so than truth. As James Clear wrote, "Convincing someone to change their mind is really the process of convincing them to change their tribe."

Changing your tribe may seem like a herculean task, but there's value in seeing reality more objectively. Clear thought prevents us from falling for false narratives, keeps our ego in check, and most importantly, allows us to think for ourselves.

Legendary investor Charlie Munger has an "iron prescription" to make sure he doesn't become a slave to his beliefs. "I'm not entitled to have an opinion on this subject unless I can state the arguments against my position better than the people do who are supporting it," he says. "I think only when I reach that stage am I qualified to speak."

BATTLING
BLIND BELIEF

In 2006, Sarah Edmondson paid $3,000 to participate in a five-day "executive success program" in Albany, New York. The workshop was created by NXIVM, a personal development company that boasted its "patented technology" could help ambitious people like Edmondson become more successful in their personal and professional lives.

On day three of the five-day training, Edmondson had a "breakthrough" during a session on self-esteem and limiting beliefs.

Over the next 12 years, Edmondson went on to become a top-ranking member at the company, responsible for opening a chapter in Vancouver, recruiting new members, and teaching seminars to spread the group's philosophy. She finally gained what she had been seeking—purpose and connection.

> *Convincing someone to change their mind is really the process of convincing them to change their tribe.*
>
> **JAMES CLEAR**

But she was being led down a dangerous path.

Eventually, Edmondson was told that as part of a women's empowerment initiation ritual she'd have to get a small tattoo of a Latin symbol. Along with other female NXIVM members, she was branded with the initials that belonged to the founder of the organization.

Edmondson believed she belonged to a personal development company. Instead, she had been part of a cult that engaged in sex trafficking under the guise of mentoring and empowering women. She says figuring out that the symbol bore the initials of the founder "was the biggest wake-up call." She left the organization and filed criminal complaints against the leaders.

Edmondson's story is detailed in a disturbing documentary called *The Vow*. After watching it, I couldn't stop thinking about the fallibility of the human mind and the slippery nature of identity and belief.

Barry Meier, the *New York Times* reporter who broke the NXIVM story, said, "The central thing that I took away from [this story] was how extraordinarily vulnerable we are as people, and how even people who, on the surface, are bright, capable, talented, and successful, have this intense vulnerability. That vulnerability is available for someone to exploit."

Right about now, you're probably thinking: "Oh please. I would never get roped into something like this." But ask yourself: When's the last time you challenged an institution— political, religious, even astrological? (According to the Pew Research Center, more than 60% of American millennials believe in New Age spirituality, which includes reincarnation, astrology, and psychics.)

In a dynamic, ever-changing world, we have to learn how to contend with uncertainty. And when we don't have answers, it's easy to turn to sources of authority to ease our anxiety about the future—or to see people or institutions as being authoritative, like NXIVM, when in fact they're merely manipulative.

Not every cult has branding rituals or megalomaniacal long-haired cult leaders. There are cults all around us in the form of echo chambers that we voluntarily (and sometimes involuntarily) join. From the news we trust to the social media groups in which we participate to the friends with whom we communicate, many of us absorb ideas from sources who tend to share and reaffirm our existing opinions.

Many times, we find ourselves digging our heels in the ground even when there's evidence that contradicts our belief. This feeling of believing that you *should* believe something— despite realizing it's ridiculous—is what philosopher Daniel Dennett calls "**belief in belief**."

This phenomenon isn't only reserved for religions or cults. It also appears in everyday life. Dennett explains that the entire financial system hinges on belief in belief. For instance, politicians and economists realize that a sound currency depends on people *believing* that the currency is sound—even if there's proof to show otherwise.

Why does this happen? In large part, because the human brain craves predictability, and it feels betrayed when trusted sources change their positions. To ease the discomfort, we'll go to great lengths to make sense of the inconsistency.

In 2008, Howard University psychology professor Jamie Barden conducted a study to determine how people processed inconsistent behavior of political candidates. He told a group of students—half of whom identified as Republican and half as Democrat—to judge the behavior of a hypothetical guy named Mike.

The students received the following information about Mike: He had organized a political fundraiser, had a little too much to drink, and crashed his car on the way home from the event. A month after the incident, Mike went on the radio and preached to listeners about how no one should ever drive drunk.

There's two ways to interpret Mike's behavior: 1) That he is a hypocrite or 2) that he learned and grew from his mistake. So how did the participants in the study judge Mike's actions?

Here's the key detail: Half the time Mike was described to the students as a Republican and half the time he was described as a Democrat.

When Mike was presented as being of the same political party as the study participant, only 16% of the participants judged him to be a hypocrite. But when Mike was presented as being from the opposing political party, 40% judged him to be a hypocrite.

In other words, when someone acts in unpredictable ways, we don't change our beliefs. We simply change our *interpretation* of their actions to make them more congruent with our existing beliefs.

Psychologist Philip Tetlock conducted a famous study in which he concluded that the political world is divided into two groups of people whom he calls foxes and hedgehogs. (Based on the ancient Greek aphorism, which says the fox knows many things, but the hedgehog knows one big thing.)

Tetlock says that some leaders behave like hedgehogs: They have one big worldview based on what they see as a few fundamental truths, and these people are highly consistent. So a free-market hedgehog uses the lens of the free market to understand all types of different things. The foxes, on the other hand, tend to be very inconsistent because they are guided by drawing on many diverse strands of evidence and ideas.

So Tetlock conducted a massive study over 20 years to look at how accurate "foxes" and "hedgehogs" were in predicting what the future was going to look like. In the end, he found that over time, foxes tend to be much more accurate than hedgehogs.

Why? Because for a fox, being wrong is an opportunity to learn new things, so they are much better equipped to deal with the complex and unpredictable things life throws their way.

Tetlock's work has challenged the idea of what it means to be an expert. We may think of experts as these knowledgeable figures who are entrenched in their beliefs and never flip-flop. Rather, Tetlock says, the experts whose predictions often turn out correct are those who frequently use terms like "but," "however," and "although."

That's why cult leaders are often described as charismatic and persuasive—they present the world in black-and-white terms with little room for nuance.

After leaving NXIVM, Edmondson became more mindful of the information she consumed on a daily basis. She began to inquire and embrace skepticism in an effort to get closer to the truth. "I'm at the point where I will never follow something blindly," Edmondson said. "I have to know why I'm doing what I'm doing, because I did follow blindly for 12 years, and look where it got me."

Approaching the world with a healthy dose of intellectual humility and skepticism is a good thing—even if it may not be popular. As historian Daniel J. Boorstin said, "The greatest obstacle to discovery is not ignorance—it is the illusion of knowledge."

ROB HENDERSON,
Author

Rob Henderson coined the term "luxury beliefs," which he defines as ideas and opinions that confer status on the wealthy, while inflicting costs on everyone else.

Take the idea that "monogamy is outdated," for instance. "Saying monogamy is outdated will give you some social cred from other elite college students," he says. "And it's kind of ironic because the upper class is most likely to broadcast these kinds of unusual luxury beliefs, but then they themselves are most likely to get married, and recapitulate the privileges they are critiquing."

In other words, luxury beliefs are performative status symbols—they are popular, but fake. Luxury beliefs, like luxury clothing, signal high status. But as those "ideological fur coats," as Henderson calls them, go out of style, they leave behind tangible consequences for the disadvantaged people who often bear the brunt of "trendy" beliefs.

WILL STORR,
Journalist and novelist

Will Storr is a journalist who writes about the science of status-seeking. He says we bestow status upon people who we see as dominant, virtuous, or competent, and we begin to emulate them in hopes of becoming dominant, virtuous, or competent ourselves.

This is how we become participants in what he calls "the status game." The game works like this: We begin with a question, form a belief, and join groups that validate that belief. Once we join a tribe, we identify the most powerful high-status members and mimic their beliefs, tastes, and behaviors.

"We do this partly as a gameplay strategy: by blindly adopting the opinions and habits of the successful, we hope to become successful ourselves," Storr writes.

There are many status games we play, and it's important to know our part in them. A cancel culture mob, for example, relies on a virtue dominance game. It forces you to adhere to the rules with threat, pain, and punishment. A virtue success game, on the other hand, uses competence to increase good. Someone running a marathon to raise money for breast cancer research, for example, is playing a virtue success game.

Become more aware of what status game you're playing, and ask yourself, "What's my role, and can I use my status for good?"

STRIVING FOR INTELLECTUAL HUMILITY

Julia Galef wants you to imagine for a moment that you're a soldier in the midst of battle. You attack, you defend, you protect, but mostly you want to *win*.

Now, imagine playing a different role: a scout. Unlike the soldier, your goal as a scout isn't to defend one side over the other. Instead, you're there to understand, survey the terrain, identify threats and obstacles and come back with a map that's as accurate as possible.

She often uses the **soldier** and **scout** roles as metaphors for how all of us process information and ideas in our daily lives. The two mindsets demonstrate how clearly we see the world.

"Some pieces of information feel like our allies—we want them to win; we want to defend them. And other pieces of information are the enemy, and we want to shoot them down. That's why I call motivated reasoning 'soldier mindset,'" Galef says. "Scout mindset means seeing what's there as accurately as you can, even if it's not pleasant."

Some pieces of information feel like our allies— we want them to win; we want to defend them. And other pieces of information are the enemy, and we want to shoot them down.

JULIA GALEF

Galef is the president and cofounder of the Center for Applied Rationality, a nonprofit organization devoted to training people in strategies for reasoning and decision-making. She's the rare type of person who takes pride in changing her mind.

Let's explore several strategies that Galef recommends to help us become more rational and improve our judgment as individuals.

The first is to evalute the current state of your beliefs. In her podcast, *Rationally Speaking,* Galef often asks her guests the following questions: **"What have you changed your mind about?"** and **"What do you think are the strongest arguments against your view?"** These two questions help her subjects become intellectually honest by confronting their own preconceived beliefs and prejudices.

Next, she recommends **divorcing your beliefs from yourself.** In this visualization exercise, Galef suggests picturing the belief that you're defending in an argument as existing a few feet away from your body. "So when the person I'm talking to attacks it, I can picture the attack being directed at this thing that's not me," she says. The reason it's helpful to personify your beliefs in such a way is that it doesn't feel like a personal attack. You can then be more objective when evaluating how your belief stands up to the attack.

Third, she recommends **celebrating being objective, not right.** Congratulate yourself when you've evaluated an argument as dispassionately and fairly as possible instead of congratulating yourself on simply being right. The ultimate goal should be moving toward the truth, not validating the ego. The latter is driven by emotion, the former by rational thought.

Finally, **stop labeling your counterpart during an argument**: Oftentimes, the way we label people can lead us astray. Imagine if you could hear a political candidate's ideas coming out of the mouth of someone of another race and gender. If things (or people) were packaged differently, could we hear them differently?

Galef believes so. When you're feeling frustrated, irritated, or hostile toward a person with whom you're arguing, try this mental exercise: Take the words they say and visualize a friend or family member that you respect saying the same things. "Try to evaluate the arguments as if they're coming from someone you like more, and I think you'll find it much easier to consider them fairly than you otherwise would," she says.

Remember, changing your mind is a feature, not a bug.

ANTHONY BOURDAIN,
Renegade chef

Anthony Bourdain once said that traveling to Paris to see the Eiffel Tower is lethal to the soul.

He sought out the places off the beaten path, the ones that rip you out of your comfort zone. "We tend to be overconcerned with safety and with cleanliness in ways that stand between us," he said. He was an evangelist for street food because that's how he believed a tourist could experience the magic of local cuisine.

In other words, going rogue when you're exploring a new city is a must. Bourdain avoided the tourist traps by refusing to eat at English-speaking restaurants, finding a hole-in-the-wall eatery, pointing to whatever dish the guy next to him was eating, and being open to experimentation.

The awkward interactions with strangers who don't speak your language is where the best experiences lie. "It's those little human moments that are the ones that stick with you forever, the random acts of kindness," he said.

When visiting a new place, Bourdain believed that you learn something—not just about the place, but about yourself. "Travel isn't always pretty. It isn't always comfortable. Sometimes it hurts, it even breaks your heart. But that's OK," he said. "The journey changes you; it should change you. It leaves marks on your memory, on your consciousness, on your heart, and on your body. You take something with you. Hopefully, you leave something good behind."

After every journey, ask yourself, "What new thing did I discover about myself and what beliefs were confirmed or invalidated?"

THINKING FOR YOURSELF

To change your beliefs, you must first understand what it is *you* believe. Let me share a personal story on the challenges of independent thought.

We emigrated from Bulgaria to the United States when I was in fourth grade, and figuring out the cultural norms of my new country was tough. I didn't speak English. I used a fork and knife to cut my pizza slice at lunch. I couldn't play kickball. And I gave up all hope when I was presented with a breaded, deep-fried sausage on a stick that Americans called a "corn dog."

Every day was something new, and every day I hated that I was different.

That meant a few things. It meant eating lunch alone, and always feeling like an outsider. As an adult, I'm able to reason my way through the situation and understand why it happened. But as a nine-year-old, those experiences rewired my brain and warped my thinking for years to come.

We moved, and I got to start seventh grade with kids who didn't know me during the fork-and-knife pizza days. I still remember walking into my new school thinking, "You can be whoever you want to be here." So, naturally, I overcorrected.

Suddenly, I worshipped at the altar of conformity and conventional wisdom. I hated advice like, "Always be yourself," because being yourself, in my mind, rendered a vivid image of sitting alone at a cafeteria table. I was over-the-top nice, I never had an opinion, and I ate pizza with my bare hands like a savage. I was boring, and it was exhausting.

By the time I graduated college, I had friends, I was generally well liked, and I was never alone. But now, not only did I still feel like an outsider, I also felt like a fraud. This is referred to as **normative social influence**, a type of conformity in which a person publicly accepts the views of a group but privately rejects them. It's a pretty lonely way to live.

When I moved to New York as an adult, I got another chance to practice independent thought. In 2020, I quit my job at *Fortune* to launch my media company **THE PROFILE**, and I thought I was past conventional thinking. But you can't quit this habit cold turkey. It haunts you in weird ways.

First come the anxious questions: "Who could possibly care about my opinion?" "Which writer's style should I imitate?" "Who will ever read this thing?" But then come the questions that matter: "What is my voice?" "Why do I have to accept society's idea of what success looks like?" and "What the hell do I actually believe?"

In a blog post titled, "The Four Quadrants of Conformism," technology investor Paul Graham says most people fall into one of four categories: those who are aggressively conventional-minded, passively conventional-minded, passively independent-minded, and aggressively independent-minded.

People who are **aggressively conventional-minded** not

only believe that rules must be followed, but that those who break the rules must be punished. On the other hand, those who are **passively conventional-minded** make sure they follow the rules and worry that those who break them might be punished.

The **passively independent-minded** are those who don't really give much thought to the rules at hand. The **aggressively independent-minded** are the ones who constantly challenge the rules and often intentionally defy the authority figures who implement the rules in the first place.

"The call of the passively conventional-minded is 'What will the neighbors think?' The call of the passively independent-minded is 'To each his own,'" Graham writes. "And the call of the aggressively independent-minded is 'Eppur si muove.'" ("And yet it moves"—the phrase physicist Galileo Galilei is believed to have said to his inquisitors after he was forced to recant his assertion that the Earth moves around the Sun.)

Thinking for yourself requires a certain level of humility and acceptance that you might change your mind as you receive new information.

Galef recommends using a powerful paradigm of thinking called **The Bayes Rule,** a formula that describes the probability of an event based on prior knowledge of the conditions that might be relevant to the event.

In essence, it tells you how to weigh evidence and change your beliefs.

Here's what it looks like:

$$P(A \mid B) = \frac{P(B \mid A) \, P(A)}{P(B)}$$

Where:

- $P(A \mid B)$—the probability of event A occurring, given event B has occurred
- $P(B \mid A)$—the probability of event B occurring, given event A has occurred
- $P(A)$—the probability of event A
- $P(B)$—the probability of event B

You don't need to understand the math behind it in order to apply it to your own life.

Here's how Galef recommends you use it: Understand that your beliefs are grayscale—and that your confidence in them can fluctuate as you learn new things. Next time you think you agree with a political party 100% of the time, ask yourself: "What do I actually believe, and can these new facts help update my belief system?"

Graham suggests you use a similar mental framework that involves treating beliefs like a puzzle. Whenever someone makes an assertion as a fact, ask yourself, "Is that true?"

"The end goal is not to find flaws in the things you're told, but to find the new ideas that had been concealed by the broken ones. So this game should be an exciting quest for novelty, not a boring protocol for intellectual hygiene," he writes in a blog post called *How to Think For Yourself*. "And you'll be surprised, when you start asking 'Is this true?', how often the answer is not an immediate yes. If you have any imagination, you're more likely to have too many leads to follow than too few."

Independent thought is hard and messy and often unpopular, but it's also liberating. We trip up so many times because we care about the crowd's opinion and believe in whatever the intellectual mob deems worthy. There's a "right time" to get married, have kids, quit your job, build a company, and eat pizza with a fork and a knife.

Who decides that? Hopefully, it's *you*.

NEIL DEGRASSE TYSON,
Physicist

If someone tried to sell you crystals that promise to cure all your ailments, what would you do? Believe it outright or reject it immediately?

Neil DeGrasse Tyson says those are both intellectually lazy responses. The best defense against sloppy thinking is skepticism, which requires asking probing questions to get to the root of whether there's supporting proof to back up the claim. "A proper skeptic questions what they're unsure of but recognizes when valid evidence is presented to change their mind," he says. "It's a path of inquiry toward the truth."

He recommends invoking the scientific method in your everyday life. Tyson says that many people have lost the ability to judge what is true and what is not.

He believes we need to constantly seek out the objective truths in our world. "Do whatever it takes to ensure you do not fool yourself into thinking something is true that is actually false, or that something is false which is actually true," he says.

That involves observing, asking questions, testing your hypotheses, and coming to a logical conclusion.

If I'm asking you for your true opinion, I shouldn't give you mine first.

ANNIE DUKE

ANNIE DUKE,
Poker player

If you allow people to talk to each other, they'll pretty much always come to consensus. So if several people are interviewing a candidate for a job, it's best to have them write down their opinions about the person separately before talking to each other.

In other words, bias is infectious. "If I'm asking you for your true opinion," says decision science author and poker player Annie Duke, "I shouldn't give you mine first."

Bits of
GENIUS

Avoid becoming a slave to your beliefs by knowing the best arguments against them.

The illusion of knowledge is worse than ignorance. Skepticism and intellectual humility are not signs of weakness but strength.

We play lots of different status games—focus on what each game forces or rewards and you'll be able to avoid toxic or pointless ones.

A soldier mindset is about victory at all costs. A scout mindset is better: It's about accuracy at all costs.

Become more scout-like by contemplating moments when you've changed your mind before; divorcing your beliefs from yourself so that it hurts less when they're attacked; celebrating objectivity as an end in itself, rather than being right; and avoiding giving other people labels when arguing with them.

Beliefs are best seen as grayscale—not black and white.

Treat beliefs like puzzles. Ask: Is that true? And keep asking. It's not about finding problems in ideas but finding new ideas behind defunct or damaged ones. The process is invigorating—and effective.

Clarity is vital—but what is it in service of? Self-improvement *can* be a positive end in itself. But there's more. As we'll discover in the next chapter, the world's most successful people often build powerful communities that make a real difference. Let's see how.

Chapter Eight

BUILDING AN ENGAGED COMMUNITY

WHEN YOU THINK about loneliness, you probably don't picture a superhero.

Val Kilmer was the leading man of the 1990s, playing Batman, Iceman, Doc Holliday, and Jim Morrison. By 1995, he was raking in $6 million per film. But over the years, Kilmer became a social recluse who now admits to "feeling lonely part of every day."

Whether you're a world-famous actor or a grandmother with few social ties, loneliness is a universal human experience. But unlike solitude, it's not a particularly pleasant one.

To combat loneliness, people are turning to astrology and participating in clinical trials for a loneliness pill. In Japan—the country with the world's oldest population—lonely elderly women resort to shoplifting in search of the community and stability of jail.

We may be active on multiple social media platforms yet we're still in desperate need of human connection.

We yearn to combat loneliness and be a part of something bigger and more purposeful. So how can you strengthen your existing ties as a community member? Better yet, how can you build a loyal and engaged community of likeminded people from scratch?

COMBATING LONELINESS

When I think about loneliness, I often think back to *Rolling Stone's* profile on Elon Musk. In it, the billionaire entrepreneur discusses his marriage to writer Justine Musk, his marriage to actress Talulah Riley, and his breakup with actress Amber Heard. During the conversation, Musk shakes his head and grimaces: "If I'm not in love, if I'm not with a long-term companion, I cannot be happy."

The writer explains that needing someone so badly that you feel like nothing without them is considered codependence. Musk disagrees and says, "It's not true. I will never be happy without having someone. Going to sleep alone kills me."

There's truth to what Musk is saying, the writer notes. It is lonely at the top—but not for everyone. It's lonely at the top for those who were lonely at the bottom. So what can we do today to make sure we don't end up as anxious and lonely billionaires?

As Musk's story reveals, loneliness is sort of subjective. Yes, the quality of our relationships matters, but it's the story we tell ourselves about those relationships that matters more. Let's explore that in more detail.

First, let's discuss the difference between loneliness and solitude. You may be thinking, "But we're all part of so many social networks! How is it possible we're still in desperate need for human connection?"

Much of our isolation is self-inflicted. We long for company yet we rejoice for alone time. As comedian John Mulaney put it:

"Sometimes I'll be talking to someone, and I'll be like 'Yeah, I've been really lonely lately' and they'll be like

'Well we should hang out!' and I'm like 'No, that's not what I meant. That's not what I meant at all."

It's good to be alone, society tells us, it's *self-care*. When a friend is going through a trying time, we prescribe loneliness masquerading as empowerment. Tough breakup? Grab a copy of *Eat, Pray, Love*, and go on a month-long silent meditation retreat. Hard week at work? Pour yourself a glass of wine, cancel your plans, and binge on Netflix until you numb your mind.

Our culture sends contradictory messages because it doesn't know the difference between solitude and loneliness. Solitude helps us regulate emotions, while loneliness dulls them. John Cacioppo, a professor who studied the effects of loneliness, said, "There is a big difference between **objective isolation** and **perceived isolation,** and perceived isolation is loneliness."

I interviewed Laura Entis, a writer who has covered loneliness in its many forms for years, about the science of the condition. She explained the difference between objective and perceived isolation.

"Loneliness is perceived social isolation, or the gap between what you want your social relationships to be like and how you perceive them to be," she told me. "While it's certainly possible to be lonely when you're alone, the adage 'lonely in a crowd' can also be true. If you crave connection but don't feel close to those around you, even if you're surrounded by other people—that's still loneliness."

Entis explained that it helps to first evaluate the nature of our relationships. If we have few relationships but find them personally satisfying, then we are unlikely to feel lonely. "Loneliness only occurs when there's a discrepancy between the relationships we want and those we feel we have, which is why some people can lead truly solitary lives without being lonely," she says.

This explains how people with money, connections, and fame can find themselves in a bottomless pit of loneliness.

For instance, while he was in the NFL, Ryan Leaf valued only three things—money, power, and prestige. But after getting released from several teams, he developed a painkiller addiction, attempted suicide, and committed burglary.

What saved his life? A 32-month prison sentence. It wasn't until he went to the prison library and began teaching inmates to read that he woke up from his haze. "You'll feel like for the first time in your life that you're doing something for somebody else," he writes. "That it's not all about you. And your narcissism will start to wane."

There's something to this.

Steve Cole is a UCLA professor whose research suggests that one of the most effective ways to break the cycle of chronic loneliness is to pursue a goal or a sense of purpose larger than yourself, ideally one that requires you to interact and cooperate with other people.

"Maybe it's volunteering. Maybe it's searching for spirituality. Maybe it's simply completing a meaningful project at work," Entis says. "Focusing on a shared vision—particularly one that you care deeply about—helps distract us from the lonely brain's hypercritical loops, allowing us to let our guard down and build new connections."

In other words, we can combat loneliness by building a community with strong social ties.

But here's the thing: We already exist in a world with countless communities. It's not only community we're seeking—it's belonging, loyalty, and meaning.

JAMES CLEAR,
Author of Atomic Habits

Author James Clear has been studying habits for years, and his most profound finding is that true behavior change lies in *identity* change. And our identities can shift in different social contexts.

This is why Clear emphasizes the need to join a group of people that promotes collaboration over competition. "Forget about the comparison and try to find peers that you can connect with, collaborate with, and [you'll] rise together," he told me. "The more that you can join groups where your desired behavior is the normal behavior, it starts to become this powerful rising tide where you can succeed side by side rather than in conflict."

BRYAN STEVENSON,
Cofounder of the
Equal Justice Initiative

Bryan Stevenson has been called "the death row lawyer" because in the last 30 years Stevenson and his staff have won the release of more than 135 wrongly condemned prisoners on death row.

Stevenson litigates on behalf of society's most vulnerable—juvenile offenders, people wrongly convicted, and poor people denied effective representation. There are injustices committed every day, but we don't see them simply because we are confined to a single, sheltered community.

To better understand other perspectives, Stevenson

The
difference
between an
audience and a
community is
which way the
chairs are
facing.

CHRIS BROGAN

recommends stepping outside of your existing community and visiting a shelter, volunteering at a food bank, or helping someone going through a tough time.

"We must get proximate to suffering and understand the nuanced experiences of those who suffer from and experience inequality," he writes in his book *Just Mercy.* "If you are willing to get closer to people who are suffering, you will find the power to change the world."

BUILDING LOYALTY

In a hyperconnected world, we point to our social media followings and tout our abilities to "build a community of loyal followers."

That's a misuse of the word. We say "community" when we mean "audience." How do you know the difference? Author Chris Brogan puts it perfectly: "The difference between an audience and a community is which way the chairs are facing."

So if you're wondering whether you have built an audience or a community (no matter how small), ask yourself: Am I communicating in one direction where people are only listening to me or are the conversations often dynamic and happening in a circle between multiple people?

Audience refers to the group of people who may be interested in the content you produce—they consist of the people who listen to your podcast, who read your newsletter, or who follow you on Twitter. Your **community** consists of likeminded people who are driven by a mutual purpose or interest and they devour the content that you produce while also interacting with you and other community members on a regular basis.

When you think about the most rabid online communities, who do you think of? Lady Gaga's "Little Monsters." Beyonce's "Beyhive." Taylor Swift's "Swifties." These are all devoted cult-like fan communities that may seem like they're an audience but they're actually micro-communities all on their own.

Let's start with Lady Gaga. When she was starting her career as an artist, she was working with talent manager Troy Carter. She and Carter developed a philosophy called "The First 50," which referred to finding the first 50 most loyal fans.

Lady Gaga first became popular in New York's LGBTQ community, so she played four to five clubs a night to make sure that her most loyal fans felt connected to her on a personal level. Gaga engaged with fans on social media, met them at her performances, and took their feedback. Instead of focusing on audience like many of her peers, Gaga focused first on building a community that shared her values.

The ties became stronger, and ultimately, her "superfan" base snowballed into hundreds of millions of fans around the world. Here's how Carter explained Gaga's growth strategy: "It's the slow bake versus the microwave."

Taylor Swift is also a master at building loyalty among her fans around the globe.

She finds her biggest and most loyal fans and makes them feel like they're the most important people in the room. In the lead-up to her albums *1989* and *Reputation,* she created a series of events called "Secret Sessions" where she personally scoured the internet for her most loyal fans and invited them to a listening session in her *own home.*

Swift made them cookies, played her newest songs before their release, and took photos with each of the attendees. Another time, she chose a number of fans, learned a little about them from their social media profiles and sent them personalized presents. She even surprises her fans at their own weddings. Although you may argue these acts of goodwill aren't scalable, they are the key to humanizing a brand and building lifelong loyalty.

Of course, these are celebrities who want to humanize their brand and build loyalty among their fan bases. But the reason I give these examples is to show how the audience of an artist is actually made up of micro-communities formed around a shared interest (the love for an artist's music).

So what does this mean on a smaller scale? When you're building a community from scratch, you'll want to do three key things that build lifelong loyalty: 1) **overserve your community members**; 2) **build goodwill;** and 3) **create moments of serendipity.**

Let me give you an example of something I did when I first started my newsletter **THE PROFILE**. The newsletter was still relatively small, and I saw the occasional tweet of support, but there wasn't any *real* community around it. I had never met my readers in person.

So in 2019, I sent an email to my subscriber list that read:

"I believe that the antidote to loneliness is community, and this newsletter is living proof of it. I have the most interesting and thoughtful conversations with you guys every week. It's truly a shame we can't all just meet in the same place for one day to share ideas face-to-face. So I want to do an experiment that could change that."

I spent a week building a spreadsheet matching people by city, emailing them individually, and sending calendar invites. Ultimately, readers met up on the same weekend in December *all over the world.*

We held meetups in New York, San Diego, London, Singapore, Mumbai, and Nairobi. The readers all chose different activities—some went to a wine bar, others headed to an art museum, and others got together for a picnic.

When I asked the subscribers *why* they were interested in meeting fellow newsletter readers in person, many of the responses began with: "I've been feeling lonely..." Many of them were seeking to connect with other curious people who shared their interests.

The meetups weren't large—some only had two or three participants. But the reason they were successful is because the encounters were meaningful. As the organizer, I **overserved** the community by personally emailing and matching fellow readers across the world; **built goodwill** by attending the meetup in New York City; and **created moments of serendipity** for the readers who would've never connected otherwise.

After the meetup, one reader who participated in the Kenya event emailed me and said, "We met up as readers, and ended up as friends."

Remember, community isn't about follower count or audience size. Community is about connecting and building loyalty among people whose paths may have never crossed otherwise.

MARC LORE,
Serial entrepreneur

When starting a business, Marc Lore says, you want to aim for obsession. "Building something that customers love is the hardest part and then, later, you can work backward to get to a profit," he says.

When he started Diapers.com, he was solving a big problem for overwhelmed parents who wanted diapers delivered fast without paying a markup. The company guaranteed boxes of diapers, overnight, at equivalent pricing, with a 365-day return policy and immediate answers to customer queries, all without a membership fee.

"The experience didn't just create a buying preference, it created an emotional connection with our brand," he says. But getting to that kind of experience could not come with immediate profit. "It can seem intimidating and risky to bet on a longer-term return, but in reality, it is much riskier to put money and time into something that customers think is just so-so," he says.

Get out of the "friend zone" with your customers by making sure they are head-over-heels in love with your product.

FORMING AN EMOTIONAL CONNECTION

The *Humans of New York* comment section has been called "the nicest place on the internet."

As photographer Brandon Stanton publishes moving portraits on his page, the people in his digital community actively engage with his work, posting kind and uplifting comments.

In 2012, the page had 64,000 fans. A decade later, the community has grown to more than 20 million people on social media.

But Stanton has successfully built a community on the internet *and* in the real world through his hidden genius: Using empathy as a tool for good. He discovered early on that the very bedrock of community-building is about **forming an emotional connection** with your community members.

It's no secret that *Humans of New York* owes part of its success to Facebook's algorithm. "For years and years and years, I posted four photos a day, every single day," he told me. "And this is when *Humans of New York* was dovetailing with the rise of Facebook."

In 2012, Facebook conducted a study in which its data scientists manipulated the news feeds of 689,003 users. One set of users saw only negative posts for a full week, whereas the other set of users saw only positive posts. The goal was to measure how this affected their moods.

What the data scientists discovered was evidence of **emotional contagion**. Just like you can catch a bad cold, you can catch a bad mood.

"When positive expressions were reduced, people produced fewer positive posts and more negative posts; when negative expressions were reduced, the opposite pattern occurred," according to the paper published in the scientific journal, *The Proceedings of the National Academy of Sciences*. "These results indicate that emotions expressed by others on Facebook influence our own emotions, constituting experimental evidence for massive-scale contagion via social networks."

Humans of New York benefited from this emotional contagion, and its intimate stories of strength, redemption, and love were enough to help the page's fans form an emotional bond to the subjects being profiled as well as to *Humans of New York* itself. "We connect much more to each other's pains than we do our successes," Stanton said.

And then "Tanqueray" happened. In 2020, Stanton published a moving 32-post narrative on Stephanie Johnson, a 76-year-old woman who worked as a burlesque dancer named Tanqueray in the 1970s.

To really know pain in other people is to know yourself in them.

BRANDON STANTON

Her health had recently taken a bad turn, so Stanton created a GoFundMe to cover her medical costs. Moved by her story, more than 100,000 complete strangers in the *Humans of New York* community donated a whopping $2.7 million in a matter of weeks.

In other words, if the emotion is powerful enough, it can drive people to *act*.

As researcher Steve Cole's work suggests: Combating loneliness lies in pursuing a goal larger than yourself. In a divided political atmosphere, the Tanqueray campaign united complete strangers from all over the world who were eager to help a fellow human in a meaningful way.

So how can you make your community members emotionally invested?

Authenticity.

Stanton's subjects regularly bare their souls to the *Humans of New York* community. But it goes further than that— Stanton *himself* shared the gritty details of the unorthodox way in which he became friends with Tanqueray, explained the seriousness of her health condition, and outlined how the money would be spent.

Loneliness exists within us all, and strangers act as mirrors in which we see our own imperfect reflections. As we become emotionally invested in those strangers' stories, we build a tight-knit community predicated on a larger purpose.

"To really identify with somebody and have compassionate empathy for them is to identify pain in others—the same pain that you've felt even though it might not have the same causes," Stanton told me. "I think that is why the story of other people's struggles and the story of Tanqueray's struggles, in particular, tapped in to such a nerve. To really know pain in other people is to know yourself in them."

CHRISTINA TOSI,
Founder of Milk Bar

Christina Tosi turned her hobby of making cookies into a multimillion-dollar business: Milk Bar, a wildly successful dessert empire that attracts customers from all over the world.

The success of any restaurant or bakery, she believes, is to emotionally connect with the customer through the experience of food. Milk Bar aims to evoke a feeling of nostalgia and playfulness through flavor, texture, and aesthetic.

And when people are emotionally invested in a brand, they transform from customers to community members. Because of this, they feel empowered to hold a company and its leaders accountable when they see wrongdoing or mistakes.

A dessert named Crack Pie was one of the core offerings that helped skyrocket Milk Bar to mass popularity. In 2019, Tosi's bakery faced backlash for its use of the name—a joke about the addictive nature of the pie and a reference to the crack cocaine epidemic of the 1980s and 1990s, which disproportionately affected Black communities.

Rather than issuing a press release, she wrote a letter directly to Milk Bar's community, explaining that the name would be changed to Milk Bar Pie. Tosi understood the importance of listening to the community, accepting their criticism, adjusting the company's actions, and taking personal responsibility.

RON FINLEY,
The "gangster gardener"

———————

Ron Finley's journey to improving his community began with a single emotion: Anger.

In 2010, he looked around his neighborhood and noticed it was littered with liquor stores, fast-food restaurants, and vacant lots. He didn't like how it looked, so he decided to take matters into his own hands.

But his mission was short-lived because he got in trouble with the law for... gardening. He had planted fruit and vegetables on the tiny strip of land between his house and the street in South Central Los Angeles. Someone complained that he was violating L.A. Code, and the city gave him a citation with an ultimatum: Remove your garden or the citation will turn into a warrant.

So Finley decided to fight it. Not only did he earn permission to continue gardening, but the city changed the law and encouraged him to build more gardens in low-income "food deserts" in neighboring communities.

He channeled his anger into a larger purpose, which is that "growing your own food gives you power. Once you have it, it's something that never can be taken from you."

Bits of
GENIUS

The quality of our relationships matter, but the stories we tell ourselves about those relationships have a huge impact too.

The difference between solitude and loneliness is the difference between objective and perceived isolation.

Doing things for others is an excellent cure for loneliness. Pursue a purpose larger than yourself—find a shared vision. It distracts us from the brain's hypercritical loops.

Join a group of people focused on collaboration over competition.

Audience and community are not the same thing. The latter is much more powerful. Some of the world's most popular artists started by seeking to build communities rather than audiences.

Build a community by overserving its members; forging goodwill; creating moments of serendipity.

Empathy is a tool for good.

Forming an emotional connection is at the heart of community. And authenticity is at the heart of emotional connection.

You don't just want to create your own community, of course. You want to be part of others'—and a truly discerning and engaged content consumer, able to cut through the noise and get the most out of what you read and watch. The world's most successful people have some interesting tactics for that too.

Chapter Nine

OPTIMIZING YOUR CONTENT DIET

ONE OF THE biggest realizations I've had in the last few years is simple but overlooked: What you eat is who you are, and *what you read is who you become.*

While most of us are willing to invest in our health, we often neglect our "content diet"—the information we feed our brains with on a daily basis.

For context, the average American used to spend an average of 11 hours a day consuming media. But in recent years, that average has reached a record high of more than 13 hours a day.

It's easy to fall into a spiral of consuming junk food content, sensationalist articles and social media posts that plunge you into destructive thought patterns. So can we inch toward leading healthier lives by optimizing what our bodies *and* our brains ingest? How do the world's most successful people do it?

UPGRADING YOUR MENTAL SOFTWARE

When SpaceX CEO Elon Musk talks about the mind, he likens it to a computer.

There's our mental "hardware," which is the raw intelligence and natural talents we're born with, and then there's our mental "software," our belief systems and thought patterns. The software, he believes, is the most important tool we possess as human beings.

In a tweet, Musk suggests that people need to develop better "mental firewalls for the information constantly coming at us," adding that a course on critical thinking should be a requirement in middle school. "Who wrote the software running in your head? Are you sure you actually want it there?"

And that exact framework is Musk's hidden genius. He's a master at upgrading the software in his brain on a regular basis by seeking and ingesting quality information. If you think about it like an iPhone, we may all possess the same *hardware*, but if we don't regularly update it to run on the latest *software*, we'll get left behind. (That's why it seems as though some of our brains are running on iOS 15 while others are still stuck on iOS 7.)

But here's the caveat: Indulging in trashy reality TV or bad rom-coms every so often isn't what slows down your software. Rather, it's the long-term consumption of mediocre content.

In something he calls the **"theory of maximum taste,"** *New York Times* columnist David Brooks says that each person's mind is defined by its upper limit—the best content that it habitually consumes and is capable of consuming.

"This theory is based on the idea that exposure to genius has the power to expand your consciousness," he writes in a column titled, "A Commencement Address Too Honest to Deliver in Person." "If you spend a lot of time with genius, your mind will end up bigger and broader than if you spend your time only with run-of-the-mill stuff."

In college, you're forced into putting quality ideas into your brain. You get tough assignments, and you have to write essays in which you argue a point you may or may not agree

"Who wrote the software running in your head? Are you sure you actually want it there?

ELON MUSK

with. After we leave college, however, many of us simply stop learning. We stop reading. We stop generating ideas.

"We get caught up in stuff, settle for consuming Twitter and, frankly, journalism," Brooks writes. "Our maximum taste shrinks. Have you ever noticed that 70 per cent of the people you know are more boring at 30 than they were at 20?"

Think about this question for a second: Is the upper limit of your mind lower than it used to be in college? If you do an honest audit of your content consumption, you'll find the answer.

BRUNELLO CUCINELLI,
Fashion mogul

The book that changed Brunello Cucinelli's life is *Meditations* by Marcus Aurelius. "I re-read it all the time—just the other day, in fact," he says. "When I was 25, I'd underline certain parts of it, in my 30s other parts, and now that I'm in my 50s, it's a completely different read."

By re-reading books at different points in your life, you notice things you may have otherwise missed.

CONDUCTING A CONTENT AUDIT

In 2019, I made a conscious decision to elevate the information I was consuming, and it had a tremendous effect on my mental state.

First, I conducted **a content audit:** I took an honest look at the content I consumed on a daily basis. What do I read? What do I watch? What do I listen to? Who do I hang out with?

Then, I made a few rules: I would read fewer surface-level news articles and more long-form profiles. I would watch less reality TV and more documentaries. I would limit my conversations to 10% small talk and 90% substance.

Finally, I made it practical. I deleted a few social media apps from my phone. I stopped mindlessly scrolling. I used Pocket and Notion to save interesting articles, podcasts, and video interviews I wanted to watch.

I joined communities and engaged with people who enjoyed brainstorming and debating new ideas. I listened to high-quality podcasts during my runs. I launched **THE PROFILE** Dossier, a weekly deep-dive that allowed me to take a closer look at a person whose life path I found interesting. I also started conducting interviews to have more compelling conversations.

If you go about your day without a content strategy, you run the risk of falling into an echo chamber full of one-sided opinions. On the internet, we are part of social media platforms that often confirm our existing beliefs. If you type a question into Google, you're served the most popular queries.

So how do you discover new content that will cultivate fresh new ideas?

Author Malcolm Gladwell says you need to create an environment that facilitates falling into "intellectual rabbit holes."

Here's how he suggests you do this: First, take a walk through towns or buildings that pique your curiosity and notice things you haven't noticed before. Next, go to the library, identify books you've liked reading in the past, and look around them on the shelf to discover something new. Finally, look at the footnotes in books or articles because they often lead you to other sources that can help you learn the subject more intimately.

When it comes to your brain, you need to get off autopilot.

SHONDA RHIMES,
Showrunner, writer, and executive producer

Over the years, Shonda Rhimes has learned how to cultivate a group of friends and peers who inspire her to be the best version of herself.

"My vision has become razor sharp," she writes in her book *Year of Yes.* "I now work to see people, not as I'd rewrite them, but as they have written themselves. I see them for who they are. And for who I am with them."

Because it's not just about surrounding yourself with people who treat you well, it's also about surrounding yourself with people whose "self-worth, self-respect and values inspire [you] to elevate [your] own behavior."

Rhimes emphasizes the importance of identifying your weaknesses and finding people with complementary skills who can help cover your blind spots. For example, she says she's not a natural-born leader and was never trained to run a company. So in order to run her company, she hired people whose strengths she felt were her weaknesses.

A large portion of our content diet is determined by the people whose opinions we value and words we absorb.

JON KABAT-ZINN,
Founder of MBSR (mindfulness-based stress reduction)

An important component of conducting a content audit is to identify the distractions present throughout your day. Mindfulness master Jon Kabat-Zinn says we're living in the age of distraction, and it's important to learn to enter the domain of awareness.

How can you do this?

Begin by going to your phone's settings and checking your screen time. How many hours per day does it say you spend scrolling through your device? Better yet, how many times a day does it say you pick up your phone? On average, people check their phones about 344 times a day (that's once every four minutes).

If you have some down time, resist the urge to scroll, swipe, or shop your boredom away. Try running without music, going on a walk without your phone, or just quietly observing your surroundings.

We think we are in this one-room house. Books help us realize we are in a mansion. Reading is a way to find the lost parts of us.

MATT HAIG

CHOOSING WHAT YOU INJECT INTO YOUR MIND

Tara Westover was 17 years old when she set foot in a classroom for the first time.

Born to survivalist Mormon parents in the mountains of Idaho, she grew up isolated from mainstream society. Her father had a severe mistrust of the government to the point where he forbade the family from visiting hospitals or attending school.

Westover's turbulent home life turned violent. She was emotionally and physically abused by her older brother. She had to break free. Education would be her escape.

Westover taught herself enough algebra to pass college entrance exams and became a competitive applicant to Brigham Young University. There, she studied history and learned for the first time about world events like the Holocaust and the civil rights movement.

When Westover was growing up, she considered her father's opinion the definition of the truth. In her family, it was understood and accepted that men have power and influence, women are submissive, and higher education is a waste of time.

As a result, she realized she held racist, homophobic, and sexist views. The only way Westover says she was able to change her mind was that people allowed her to express her beliefs out loud, which taught her she never wanted to say those words again.

"They weren't really my words," she says. "They came from somewhere else."

Westover had adopted her father's views about the world. In other words, she had downloaded his software into her own brain. It wasn't until she went to college that she asked herself a version of the question Musk asked: "Who wrote the software running in your head?"

As she began reading new material and debating the ideas she had taken for granted, Westover began *choosing* what she allowed into her brain. "The skill I was learning was a crucial one, the patience to read things I could not yet understand," she says.

There's something to this. Author Matt Haig says that reading can be a form of therapy. After he began having suicidal thoughts at age 24, Haig moved back in with his parents and used books he had read as a teenager to distract himself from his mental turmoil.

Reading then led him to the cathartic experience of writing. "Books can save your life," he says. "People don't just read books for escape. We read to find new paths for ourselves. We think we are in this one-room house. Books help us realize we are in a mansion. Reading is a way to find the lost parts of us."

After conducting a content audit as outlined in the previous section, start with **rearranging your physical environment** to make it more conducive for generating ideas. When I spoke with James Clear, he told me that he had 17 books on his desk. "I try to sprinkle good sources of information all around," he says.

He has books on his desk, next to his bed, and on top of the coffee table in the living room. "I'm never far from a good idea," he said. "Most of them aren't mine, but they're always there for me to build upon and soak up and think about and iterate on. That's how I think about optimizing my environment for having good ideas."

Remember, ideas are the lifeblood of human progress—

and those ideas aren't typically found in the mainstream. As author Haruki Murakami said, "If you only read the books that everyone else is reading, you can only think what everyone else is thinking."

EDITH EVA EGER,
Psychotherapist and Holocaust survivor

What you put into your brain directly affects how you think and how you act. When Edith Eva Eger and her family were on the train to Auschwitz, her mom told her: "We don't know where we're going, we don't know what's going to happen, but no one can take away from you what you put in your own mind."

Every time she felt despair, she tried to imagine a better reality that would inject joy into her brain. Your thoughts determine how you feel and who you become.

TOM BRADY,
NFL quarterback

Inflammation refers to your body's process of fighting against things that harm it in an attempt to heal itself. And Tom Brady believes there are a number of ways you can harm it—through injury, unhealthy food, even toxic thoughts.

"It's pretty simple—you gotta limit inflammation in the body whether it's through diet, nutrition, or your thoughts," he says. A balanced diet applies to both food *and* content.

You gotta limit inflammation in the body whether it's through diet, nutrition, or your thoughts.

TOM BRADY

Bits of
GENIUS

Make sure you ask yourself: Who wrote the software running in your head? It's easy to find a bunch of stuff installed that shouldn't really be there.

You can upgrade your mental software on a regular basis by seeking and ingesting quality information.

Your mind is defined by its upper limit—the best content that it habitually consumes and is capable of consuming.

To improve your content diet, start with a content audit: Take an honest look at the content you consume on a daily basis. What do you read? What do you watch? What do you listen to? Who do you hang out with?

To find new ideas, go down intellectual rabbit holes—follow your curiosity, embrace serendipity, see where it takes you. Deliberately wander in mind and body.

Arrange your physical environment to encourage new ideas. Surround yourself with books and other objects that inspire new trains of thought.

Go off the beaten path and consume unfashionable things or you'll end up thinking the same way as everyone else.

If ideas are the lifeblood of human progress, have you ever thought about what idea you embody? Our identity can be easily overlooked. But within it lies a realm of possibilities.

Chapter Ten

DISCOVERING YOUR HIDDEN GENIUS

Human beings are works in progress that mistakenly think they're finished.

DAN GILBERT

HERE'S A MIND-BENDING fact: Biologically speaking, the person you are today is not the person you were in your childhood. Most of your body parts have regenerated over the years—the lining of your stomach renews every few days, your bones every decade.

This is a classic example of "The Ship of Theseus Paradox," a thought experiment that raises the question of whether an object which has had all its components replaced remains fundamentally the same object. If you replace every single part of a wooden ship gradually over time, does it remain the same ship or is it a completely new vessel?

Is it your body, your mind, your outlook, your achievements, your relationships, or your possessions that define your identity? Which "you" do you consider the real you? The person you are today? Tomorrow? Ten years ago? Ten years from now?

In his TED Talk, psychologist Dan Gilbert makes the following observation: "Human beings are works in progress that mistakenly think they're finished. The person you are right now is as transient, as fleeting and as temporary as all the people you've ever been. The one constant in our lives is change."

In other words, it's possible to be the *creator* of your identity—the person you are today does not have to be the person you become tomorrow.

After studying the paths of so many successful people, there's one question left to answer: What does your *own* hidden genius look like? And how can you unlock it?

REJECTING LABELS

In 2018, I attended a start-up conference, and one of the organizers helped me find my seat. It was really loud, and all I heard him say was that I would be sitting next to "David ... *something something* ... you know, the NRA." And I thought, "Oh, the National Rifle Association? I don't know anything about guns, but here we go."

I immediately jumped to conclusions about what David must be like as a person, where his politics might lie, and what types of things he would want to talk about.

But he surprised me. David asked about my job, we chatted about the conference, and he helped me find the agenda in my conference booklet. "David from the NRA" was incredibly pleasant, and we had a lovely conversation. The topic of guns didn't come up a single time.

Several months later, I was sitting in a coffee shop when I came across an article with a picture of David in it. My initial reaction was, "Oh my God, what is 'David from the NRA' doing in *Sports Illustrated?*"

The headline was: "David Stern Is Not Looking Back." Turns out I had misheard. My seatmate was the late David Stern, former commissioner of the NBA, which is *quite* different from the National Rifle Association.

But I had done what we all do—judged and labeled. There are many labels we can sort through, ranging from political affiliation to occupation to cultural background to socioeconomic level. Sometimes, we voluntarily label ourselves, and sometimes society labels us. When we do it, labeling can act as a compass to our values. When someone else does it, a label can be a lifelong prison sentence.

In the 1930s, linguist Benjamin Whorf proposed the hypothesis of **linguistic relativity**. He believed that the words we use to describe what we see are not mere labels: they actually end up determining our reality and view of the world.

Army veteran Noah Galloway knows the destructive nature of labels better than most.

Three months into his second deployment in Iraq, Galloway was driving a Humvee when the vehicle ran over a tripwire that detonated a roadside bomb large enough to throw the entire armored vehicle through the air and into a canal adjacent to the road.

Galloway woke up in a hospital room and discovered all that he had lost. The roadside bomb had taken his left arm, left leg, and military career.

Suddenly, Galloway was back in his home in Alabama with a new label: Wounded veteran. The physical injuries were obvious, but it was the mental ones that really haunted him. He fell into a deep depression and began drinking heavily.

"You want to take pride in being a veteran, and no one wants to talk ill of veterans, but let's be real, no one's hiring us because of the way we're labeled," he told me, adding that movies often portray veterans as broken and mentally unstable.

Social media only exacerbates the problem. We label people as fixed characters—incapable of change. Entire swaths of people become "addicts," "racists," "socialists," and "criminals."

Robert Hoge has had a label attached to him since the day he was born: "Ugly."

When he was born, the first thing his mom Mary asked the doctors was: "Is my baby okay?"

He wasn't. Hoge, Mary's fifth child, was born with a tumor in the middle of his face and two severely mangled legs. Doctors suspected an anti-depressant she took when she was pregnant caused Hoge's birth defects.

Even though he got a chance at life, it wasn't easy. He spent the majority of his childhood at hospitals where doctors attempted surgery after surgery to remove the tumor. The procedures left Hoge with severe deformities on his face.

In school, he was taunted with a roster of nicknames like "toothpick legs," "transformer," "Pinocchio," "toe nose," "stumpy," and "Jake the Pig." But one day, Hoge realized something: Ugliness itself can be beautiful. The paradox lies in that beauty is *subjective*—it means different things to different people.

"My ugliness is a big part of who I am," he writes in his memoir, *Ugly*. "If you try to separate me from my scars before even engaging me in a discussion about the issue, I may as well have never existed in the first place."

And Hoge has done something that he suggests we all do: **Reclaim and reframe** the labels society has attached to you. Hoge took the word "ugly" and used it as an opportunity to tell his story.

We can move past labels by starting to see the world through what I call a **curiosity filter**, an outlook driven by asking questions and listening with purpose.

By ignoring people's differences, Hoge told me that we close ourselves off to conversations that would bring us closer together. Some of the best conversations he's had started with someone asking: "This might seem rude, but can I ask about your face/nose/scars/bumps?"

"A real key for me has been understanding that curiosity isn't

Definitions belong to the definers, not the defined.

TONI MORRISON

necessarily judgment," Hoge told me. "Sometimes it can be, but often, curiosity is just curiosity."

Remember, every time you slap a label on someone without being curious about their experience, you filter what you see. You make your world smaller, simpler, and less reflective of reality. As novelist Toni Morrison once wrote, "The definitions belong to the definers, not the defined."

KATIE ARNOLD,
Author and ultra-athlete

Katie Arnold has an interesting technique for getting rid of the labels: Find an activity that allows you to let go of your ego. She believes it's important to be able to do something that frees us of all of the identities imposed on us by society.

"I'm a writer and a runner and a mother and a reader. I'm a wife, dreamer, athlete, lover of mountains and rivers and wild places," Arnold says. "Sometimes when I am running strong and free, I am none of those things. I disappear into the mountains and the run. I become the running itself."

For Arnold, running is the activity that allows her to transcend all her identities and burdens in life. "I see that it's becoming something even bigger—a spiritual practice—and it's just the beginning," she says.

The way to get out of your ego is to immerse yourself in an activity that requires your full attention and energy.

KYLE MAYNARD,
Athlete

When most people see Kyle Maynard for the first time, they likely label him an "amputee"—not a wrestler, CrossFit instructor, gym owner, MMA fighter, weightlifter, and mountaineer.

Our assumptions, judgments, and beliefs color our world in ways that hinder us from getting to know each other in meaningful ways. Maynard isn't naive to the fact that society will label him in ways that aren't accurate.

The beauty, though, is that you can't put someone like Maynard in a box. "I'm not that one thing," he says. "I'm not a speaker. I'm not an author. I'm not any one thing. I'm not even an entrepreneur. I don't care. I don't care to have any label, I'm not an amputee or a wrestler or whatever."

REALIZING WHO YOU ARE NOT

Francis Ngannou is the heavyweight champion of the world. In mixed martial arts circles, he's known as "the baddest man on the planet," and that's for good reason.

The power of his punch is unmatched. Ngannou holds the record for the hardest punch in the world after registering 129,161 units of power on a bag that measures the power of a punch.

"His punches are equivalent to 96 horsepower. That's equal to getting hit by a Ford Escort going as fast as it can," said UFC president Dana White. "It's more powerful than a 12-pound sledgehammer from full force overhead. Holy sh★t."

At six foot four inches and 257 pounds, Ngannou has a long history of developing strength—both physical and emotional.

As a child growing up in Cameroon, Ngannou endured a level of poverty few people can even imagine. After his parents divorced, he moved to his grandmother's one-room brick house with his mom and four siblings.

His family couldn't afford to buy him pen and paper for school, and he often went hungry because he'd have to skip lunch.

At age nine, Ngannou got a job digging sand mines for $1.90 per day. The work kept his body busy, but he kept his mind even busier by daydreaming of making it to America and becoming a world-famous boxer. This may sound like childhood fantasy, but Ngannou felt the reality of it in his bones.

Because of this, Ngannou's vision for his life was always at odds with the vision of his family and the elders in his village. This got him labeled as "a bad kid" when in reality he was just an ambitious kid. He was so obsessed with this dream of moving to the United States that he gave himself a nickname— "American Boy."

When he was 22, Ngannou was ready to execute on the plan that had percolated in his head for over a decade. He left the village to find a gym in a nearby city with a dream of becoming a world champion in boxing. "People thought I'd lost my mind," he told me. "But I was stubborn. I had this dream inside of me—so deep."

Even though he was a dreamer, Ngannou says he was realistic about the fact that he couldn't become a world champion by training in Cameroon. So at age 25, he sold all of his belongings and set off for Morocco, the first leg of a winding and treacherous journey to Europe, and eventually America.

Ngannou traveled a whopping 3,000 miles across the Sahara

Desert—from Cameroon to Nigeria, from Nigeria to Niger, from Niger to Algeria, and from Algeria to Morocco.

It took him 14 months to make it from Morocco to Spain, an endeavor Ngannou describes as "a hell of a journey." That's because he attempted to float on a raft full of people to a Spanish island off the coast of Morocco where he could call the Red Cross and seek asylum. But the authorities pulled him out of the water six separate times, and either dropped him back in the middle of the Moroccan desert or temporarily locked him in a Moroccan jail.

He got through this chaotic journey with a laser-focused mindset, asking himself time and time again: "What do I have to lose?" Ngannou ardently believed that this temporary pain was necessary in order for him to change the trajectory of his life.

In 2013, 26-year-old Ngannou made it to Spain, and spent time at an immigration detention center, but he knew there was light at the end of the tunnel. He had finally reached his goal of getting to Europe. Now, he needed to get to work on his next goal: becoming a professional boxer.

In his search for a boxing gym, he ended up in Paris where he slept in the stairwell of a covered parking lot. Ngannou told me, "In the last 14 months, I had been through hell, so for me, [the parking lot] was like a five-star hotel. It was a palace."

Ngannou eventually found a gym, where he caught the eye of coach Didier Carmont, who suggested he try mixed martial arts as a way to make a living before trying his hand at professional boxing.

Ngannou wasn't interested because 1) he had never heard of MMA before; and 2) his passion was boxing, which he called "a noble art."

As fate would have it, the boxing gym shut down two months later, so Ngannou joined a different gym called the MMA Factory to stay in shape.

I know that if I fail, I can start over and over and over and over. I have that skill, and you can take everything from me, but you cannot take that.

FRANCIS NGANNOU

The rest is history. In 2015, Ngannou signed with the UFC, moved to the United States, and became the world heavyweight champion in a sport he didn't even know existed just several years prior.

Part of Ngannou's hidden genius is that he learned from a young age that in order to understand who you are, **you must first understand who you are *not*.**

In Cameroon, his father had a bad reputation as a violent street fighter and abusive husband to Ngannou's mother. "If there's one person on earth that impacted my life the most, that changed my life, it's my dad," Ngannou says. "The best education I had in my life was from my dad—not by showing me what to do, but by showing me what *not* to do."

Once he vowed to do things differently, Ngnannou began **embodying a version of his ideal self.** He knew he wanted to be a professional athlete, so he began *behaving* like a professional athlete. "In Cameroon, people drink a lot of beer. A *lot*," he says. "But because I had a dream of becoming a boxer, I wanted to get myself ready to get disciplined even though I had never seen a gym in my life."

He never drank or smoked because he was embodying his ideal self—a professional athlete. As James Clear says, "I think true behavior change is really identity change." If you believe, you will ultimately start to become.

And finally, Ngannou did what all successful people do: **They bet on themselves.**

Ngannou is someone who values personal freedom, and his actions prove it. He doesn't believe that the UFC contracts are fair, and he's been vocal that the title of UFC champion does not define him. When I asked what *does* define him, he told me:

"I think I just have the DNA of betting on myself. Because if you look at the story of my life, it's [about] betting on myself. You know that quote that says, 'Sometimes, to jump farther, you have to step back?'

"I know that you have to start over sometimes, which is very hard for people. Even very talented people—they don't have the audacity; they don't have that courage to start over. And I think that makes a big difference between people.

"People are afraid of starting over. They are afraid of losing something that they already have."

Because of the winding and unpredictable nature of his life, Ngannou has learned one thing: He gives himself permission to fail because he knows he has the skills necessary to course-correct. "I know that if I fail, I can start over and over and over and over. I have that skill, and you can take everything from me, but you cannot take that."

It may sound simple and straightforward, but few people have the courage to do what Ngannou has done.

Once we've reached a certain level of success, we get comfortable and complacent. We wrap our identities around jobs, relationships, and material possessions—all things we could lose. Over time, we begin to trust ourselves less, and leave our destinies in other people's hands.

It's the one thing preventing us from unlocking our own hidden genius: *We are scared to bet on ourselves.*

MATTHEW MCCONAUGHEY,
Actor

———————

To find out who you are, Matthew McConaughey suggests you go on "an identity elimination diet." He says that the process of elimination is the first step to figuring out your true identity.

"Eliminate who you are not first, and you're going to find yourself where you need to be," he says.

For instance, do you hang out with people who constantly gossip? Do you keep going to a bar that gives you the worst hangovers the next morning? If those people and places don't bring out the best in you, quit giving them your time and energy.

"Get rid of the excess, the wasted time. Decrease your options. If you do this, you will have accidentally, almost innocently, put in front of you what is important to you by process of elimination," McConaughey says.

DOLLY PARTON,
Country music legend

In the 1970s, Elvis Presley wanted to record Dolly Parton's song, "I Will Always Love You," but his manager Colonel Tom Parker wanted half the publishing rights.

Parton said no, and she wouldn't budge on her position because she knew she was not someone who abandons her values.

"I never thought of it [as being] about being a woman or a man. I thought of it as being an artist, and a writer, and a person of a strong will," she said.

This was a boundary she wasn't willing to compromise on even though it was Elvis on the other end. "It broke my heart to say no, but I was willing to suffer that temporary disappointment and heartache than to live with something that I knew was wrong," she says.

Once you establish your foundational values, you won't be

tempted to break them in difficult situations because the promise you've made to yourself is more important than any opportunity.

BETTING ON YOURSELF

At the top of my list of biggest pet peeves is the question, "What's your five-year plan?" Not because it's a bad question and not because it comes from a malicious place, but because nothing ever turns out exactly how we plan it. At least it hasn't for me.

My five-year plan when I was a freshman in college involved graduating with a full-time job as an investigative reporter. I got my degree in journalism with zero full-time offers and a move back home to live with my mom for a year.

My five year-plan when I moved to New York was to get a stable journalism job (which everyone told me was an oxymoron). Well, that one actually kind of panned out—and once I reached my goal, I realized I wanted to do something else.

So here I was in 2020, with a firm decision that I wanted to leave a world of comfort as a reporter for *Fortune* magazine to focus on my company **THE PROFILE** full time. Needless to say, writing a newsletter while quarantined at home in the middle of a global pandemic and economic crisis was *not* part of my five-year, five-month, or five-day plan. Yet even in the middle of all this chaos and uncertainty, I still had complete confidence in my decision.

Why? Because after years of studying the world's most exceptional people, I had learned the secret to personal and professional success.

You are most powerful when you tie your identity to your own name.

What does this mean in practice? Let's conduct a thought experiment.

When someone asks, "So, what do you do?" you will likely respond with your most impressive identity. For many people, the answer is their job title. For five years, my primary identity was "Polina Marinova, writer and editor at *Fortune* magazine."

But I wasn't in control of that identity. If I ever got fired or laid off, I was at risk of losing my entire self-worth—and losing that is a recipe for psychological disaster.

The best thing I did for myself is start writing **THE PROFILE** in 2017 because it gave me another identity—one that allowed me to be fully myself. It would be the identity that I would eventually choose to embody full time.

Many of you have asked, "Well, what gave you that nudge over the edge? How did you finally make this decision to leave your job?" The truth is there were many things I thought (and overthought), but I always made my way back to Anna Quindlen's 1999 commencement speech:

"Set aside what your friends expect, what your parents demand, what your acquaintances require. Set aside the messages this culture sends, through its advertising, its entertainment, its disdain and its disapproval, about how you should behave.

"Set aside the old traditional notion of female as nurturer and male as leader; set aside, too, the new traditional notions of female as superwoman and male as oppressor. Begin with that most terrifying of all things, a clean slate. Then look, every day, at the choices you are making, and when you ask yourself why you are making them, find this answer: for me, for me. Because they are who and what I am, and mean to be.

"This will always be your struggle whether you are twenty-one or fifty-one. I know this from experience. When I quit the *New York Times* to be a full-time mother, the voices of the world said that I was nuts. When I quit it again to be a full-time novelist, they said I was nuts again. But I am not nuts. I am happy. I am successful on my own terms. Because if your success is not on your own terms, if it looks good to the world but does not feel good in your heart, it is not success at all. Remember the words of Lily Tomlin: 'If you win the rat race, you're still a rat.'"

If Sara Blakely hadn't cut the feet off a pair of pantyhose, she wouldn't have built Spanx into a billion-dollar empire. If Brandon Stanton hadn't picked up a camera after getting fired from his finance job, *Humans of New York* wouldn't touch millions of lives every day. If I hadn't started sending a tiny email newsletter in 2017, you wouldn't be reading this book right now.

Remember, there is no bad time to bet on yourself. Start a newsletter, a passion project, or a new venture that lets you tie your identity to something that actually matters—your own name. Nothing is more liberating.

As a wise philosopher named Beyoncé once said, "I don't like to gamble, but if there is one thing I'm willing to bet on, it's myself."

KOBE BRYANT,
NBA legend

When he was a young player, Kobe Bryant says he went to "G.O.A.T. Mountain" to speak to players like Magic Johnson, Michael Jordan, Larry Bird, Jerry West, Oscar Robertson,

If your success is not on your own terms, if it looks good to the world but does not feel good in your heart, it is not success at all. Remember the words of Lily Tomlin: "If you win the rat race, you're still a rat."

ANNA QUINDLEN

and Bill Russell. He asked them, "What did you do? What were your experiences? What was the process like for you?"

A great exercise is to ask yourself: "Who's the person living my dream life?" Identify that person, research their early life, and figure out how they got to where they are today. As Bryant said, "We're surrounded by people who do incredible things, and the information is right there for us to learn from."

Listen intently, take what you have learned, and bet on yourself.

FRANKLIN CHANG DÍAZ,
Astronaut

Astronaut Franklin Chang Díaz successfully transitioned from researcher to astronaut to entrepreneur. When he joined NASA, people tended to be either a scientist or an astronaut—rarely both.

"The astronauts were military men, and the rocket scientists designed the rockets, but they never got to fly. That division was an obstacle for me at NASA," he says. "When I first started, it was clear that being a scientist made you less likely to fly. But that didn't seem right to me, and I kept working to remain both a scientist and an astronaut. In the end, I won out."

He remained a scientist *and* flew more than any of his peers. Chang Díaz recommends emphasizing that seemingly paradoxical qualities and personality traits can be complementary. When you bet on yourself, you fundamentally understand that you can be more than one thing in life.

Bits of
GENIUS

It's possible to be the creator of your identity—the person you are today does not have to be the person you become tomorrow.

The words we use to describe what we see are not mere labels: they actually end up determining our reality and view of the world.

Every time you slap a label on someone and put them in a box, you filter what you see. You make your world smaller, simpler, and less reflective of reality.

In order to understand who you are, you must first understand who you are *not*.

Embody the version of yourself want to be; behave like you're that person already. If you believe, you become.

All successful people bet on themselves. And there is no bad time to start doing that. Create something that lets you tie your identity to something that actually matters—your own name. Nothing is more liberating, or more powerful.

Ask yourself: Who's the person living my dream life? Identify that person, research their early life, and figure out how they got to where they are today.

CONCLUSION

"HOW DO I define success?"

That's the question that changed the trajectory of my life. In January 2020, I was riding the subway home from my job at *Fortune* magazine when I read the Anna Quindlen quote mentioned in the last chapter: "I am successful on my own terms. Because if your success is not on your own terms, if it looks good to the world but does not feel good in your heart, it is not success at all."

The truth was that I didn't feel successful on my own terms. I still saw success as a measure of status, money, and achievement. I didn't realize that the universal hidden genius across many of the exceptional people I had studied was this: Success is personal.

Comedian Jerry Seinfeld describes success as the endless process of tinkering until you get as close as you can to perfection. His definition is this: "Solitude and precision, refining a tiny thing for the sake of it."

Melinda Gates, on the other hand, says her definition of success was shaped by this Ralph Waldo Emerson quote: "To know even one life has breathed easier because you have lived.

This is to have succeeded." In her case as one of the richest women on the planet, she's used her capital to back global health initiatives and support female-led businesses.

To actor Matthew McConaughey, success looks entirely different. For him, it's the measurement of five things: 1) fatherhood, 2) friendships, 3) career, 4) being a good husband, and 5) the state of his mind, body, and spirit.

He checks in to measure them every day. "I like to see whether or not I'm in the debit section or the credit section with each one," he said in a 2016 University of Houston commencement address. "Am I in the red or am I in the black?"

Say his career is taking off but his relationship with his wife is suffering. He puts more effort into being a better husband to maintain a healthy balance. "First, we have to define success for ourselves. And then we have to put in the work to maintain it," he adds.

And much of the time, it does feel like work. But I like to think of true success as the result of challenging but meaningful work.

Soccer sensation Lionel Messi has been playing soccer every single day since he was five years old, but many people turn a blind eye to the failures, the relentless persistence, and the excruciatingly long practice sessions, only to call him "an overnight success." Although Messi was just 17 years old when he became a professional footballer, his road to success wasn't easy due to a slew of health issues that stunted his growth.

Similarly, fashion mogul Tory Burch got a call from the *Oprah Show* in 2005 to make an appearance. When Oprah gave her company a shout-out as "the next big thing in fashion," Burch's website got 8 million hits the following day.

Burch used the opportunity to tell her story and gain even more media coverage for her business. You could call her lucky or you could call her opportunistic. "The media called us an overnight success," she said in a speech at Babson College. "I guess that made sense—if you didn't count the 20,000 hours we put into building the business up to that day, or the combined half a million hours we all spent learning the industry in the years before that."

The myth of the "overnight success" is just that—a myth. There are many ways to define success and even more ways to attain it, but the key ingredient to fulfillment is *action*.

As Thomas Zurbuchen, the head of NASA's Science Mission Directorate, said, "There's a huge distance between success and failure, and only a few actions that move you from one to the other."

And that's my hope for you. I hope this book motivates you to move with purpose in the direction of your goals. Most of all, I hope that I've managed to pique your curiosity about your own interests and made you rethink the definition of success.

Below, I've transformed the ten chapters into ten key questions that will help you discover your own hidden genius:

1. Chef Grant Achatz built Alinea into the best restaurant in the world by taking creative risks and pushing the boundaries of what was possible in the culinary world. **What is the biggest, boldest, most original endeavor you can conceive of?**

2. Mentally resilient people are able to endure pain, discomfort, and uncertainty for long periods of time. How? They intentionally create friction in their lives, so that their mind is better prepared for painful experiences they may have to endure in the future. **How can you introduce moments of "elective hardship" into your week?**

3. Happy couples have a ratio of five positive interactions to

every negative interaction. "A smile, a head nod, even just grunting to show you're listening—those are all positive," John Gottman says. **How many positive interactions have you and your partner had today?**

4. We are all the unreliable narrators of our life stories. When we look at our days, we're often the main character and everyone else plays a supporting role. **What could you learn if you told your personal story from the perspective of a different character in your life?**

5. The most effective leaders use a systems-based approach in which they focus on the process rather than the outcome. If the outcome is to start a business, the system is to identify a problem you can solve, form a team, create an operating plan, and test your product in the market. **In what situations can you adopt a systems-based mindset?**

6. To make good decisions in times of uncertainty, you need to first understand the difference between reversible and irreversible decisions. If a decision is reversible, you can make it quickly without a ton of prior information—and you'll probably learn a lot more by doing it. If a decision is irreversible, however, you should be slow, deliberate, and analytical before making it. **Before making an important decision, ask yourself: Is the decision I'm about to make reversible or irreversible?**

7. Clear thought keeps us from falling for false narratives, keeps our ego in check, and most importantly, allows us to think for ourselves. Understand that your beliefs are grayscale—and that your confidence in them can fluctuate as you learn

new things. **What is one area of your life where you could examine and update your existing beliefs?**

8. Community is the antidote to loneliness. Research suggests that one of the most effective ways to break the cycle of chronic loneliness is to pursue a goal or a sense of purpose larger than yourself, ideally one that requires you to interact and cooperate with other people. **What is a meaningful activity or project you can pursue to better your own community?**

9. In something he calls "the theory of maximum taste," columnist David Brooks says that each person's mind is defined by its upper limit—the best content that it habitually consumes and is capable of consuming. **How can you improve your content diet this year?**

10. All successful people bet on themselves—and there is no bad time to start. Create a newsletter, a passion project, or a new venture that lets you tie your identity to something that actually matters—your own name. **What is something you can create *today* that allows you to tie your identity to your name?**

I want to sincerely thank you for joining me on this journey. As a big believer in people-focused learning, I would love to learn from you too. Let me know how you've applied the techniques in this book to discover your own hidden genius. You can find me at www.readtheprofile.com.

Polina

ACKNOWLEDGMENTS

Writing is a solitary endeavor, but I believe nothing of value is ever created alone. I want to take the time to thank the people who were instrumental in helping make this book a reality.

To my daughter, who was only three months old when I started writing. I had been thinking about writing a book for years but never got around to it. When she came along, everything changed. I had no time, yet I wanted to do more. This book was written in the edges of time—often found in between diaper changes, 20-minute naps, and games of peek-a-boo. I wouldn't trade a single moment with you, and I thank you for being my inspiration for writing this book. My hope for you is to find your own hidden genius much earlier than I found mine.

To my husband and partner in life, without whom this book would not exist. You took care of our daughter while I frantically wrote, you listened patiently as I read you every chapter out loud, and you offered words of encouragement when I needed them most. But, above all, you taught me to bet on myself. I'll never forget when you told me, "Never let others believe in you more than you believe in yourself." Everything we've done, we've done together.

To my parents, who sacrificed everything to move to a foreign country in pursuit of a better life. Those early years in the United States were unspeakably difficult, but I'll never forget the moments of joy and laughter along the way. Most of all, I want to thank you for encouraging me to pursue my interests—even when they didn't work out (let's all try to forget about my "acting" phase). You cheered me on when I discovered an early love for writing, when I majored in journalism, when I got my dream job at *Fortune* magazine, when I quit my dream job to pursue a newsletter full time, and when I wrote this book. Every success I've had along the way, I owe to you.

To my family and friends who feel like family, I thank you for supporting every endeavor I have embarked upon over the years. Thank you for checking in on me during the book-writing process, for giving me words of encouragement, and much-needed advice. I cherish every one of you.

To my editor Christopher Parker, who reached out with a simple, "If your thoughts ever turn to writing a book, we'd love to chat with you." That was the tiny nudge I needed to piece together the puzzle that became this book. Thank you to the Harriman House team for helping me distill my learnings into practical insights.

To my colleagues and editors at *Fortune* magazine, from whom I learned everything I know about writing. *Fortune* was my home for five years. It's the place where I grew up, both personally and professionally. I respect and look up to my fellow colleagues, whose work I still read on a daily basis.

To the reporters who wrote many of the longform profiles cited in this book. Capturing the essence of a human being is no easy task, and it's you who inspired me to launch **THE PROFILE** newsletter in the first place. *Life Stories,* a compilation of the best *New Yorker* magazine profiles, has an unforgettable line: "One of art's purest challenges is to translate a human being into words." That's exactly what you do on a daily basis, and for that I am thankful.

To the people featured in this book who were so gracious with their time and patiently answered my questions in wide-ranging interviews. You are the lifeblood of my work, and I continue to learn from you every single day.

To the readers of **THE PROFILE** who have supported me for years. I often say that **THE PROFILE** is the best community on the planet because it's full of curious, intelligent, and overall amazing humans. None of you are shy about giving me your opinions, criticisms, and feedback on a weekly basis, and you are responsible for helping improve the quality of my work.

To you, the reader of this book. A simple thank you for picking up this book and giving me some of your time. When I'm writing, I never think that someone will actually read these words, so it's an indescribable feeling to know you're holding this book in your hands right now. From the bottom of my heart, thank you.

Polina

SOURCE NOTES

In this section, I have compiled the source information for each chapter to the best of my ability. Sources have been listed in sequential order below.

Though every effort has been made to source all quotes, stories, and studies, if anything has been missed or misattributed, please email hiddengenius@readtheprofile.com, and we will make the correction.

INTRODUCTION

Craven, Mackey. "Leadership Lessons from Steve Kerr, Head Coach of the Golden State Warriors." OpenView, June 13, 2013. https://openviewpartners.com/blog/leadership-lessons-from-steve-kerr/.

Pompliano, Polina. "The Profile Dossier: Al Pacino, Hollywood's Favorite Gangster." theprofile.substack.com, May 26, 2021. https://theprofile.substack.com/p/al-pacino.

———. "The Profile Dossier: Kobe Bryant, Basketball's Greatest Storyteller." theprofile.substack.com, January 27, 2021. https://theprofile.substack.com/p/kobe-bryant.

CHAPTER 1

Achatz, Grant. "Creativity, in the Most Unexpected Places." The Atlantic, March 20,

2009. https://www.theatlantic.com/health/archive/2009/03/creativity-in-the-most-unexpected-places/1648/.

Al-Kateb, Zahra. "The Best Restaurant in the World: Alinea." Elite Traveler, April 15, 2016. https://elitetraveler.com/finest-dining/top-100-restaurants-in-the-world-old/the-best-restaurant-in-the-world-alinea-2.

Aristotle. "The Internet Classics Archive | Poetics by Aristotle." classics.mit.edu. Accessed August 10, 2022. http://classics.mit.edu/Aristotle/poetics.html?_branch_match_id=399156686146724622.

Baer, Drake. "How Shonda Rhimes Starts Her Creative Process." thriveglobal.com, November 10, 2017. https://thriveglobal.com/stories/how-shonda-rhimes-starts-her-creative-process/.

Baird, Benjamin, Jonathan Smallwood, Michael D. Mrazek, Julia W. Y. Kam, Michael S. Franklin, and Jonathan W. Schooler. "Inspired by Distraction." *Psychological Science* 23, no. 10 (August 31, 2012): 1117–22. https://doi.org/10.1177/0956797612446024.

Bruni, Frank. "Sci-Fi Cooking Tries Dealing with Reality." *The New York Times*, May 11, 2005, sec. Style. https://www.nytimes.com/2005/05/11/dining/scifi-cooking-tries-dealing-with-reality.html.

Smith LLC. "Bursting at the Seams, the Litigation Funding Industry Should Add Creativity to Its Arsenal," November 28, 2018. https://www.smithuncut.com/bursting-seams-litigation-funding-industry-add-creativity-arsenal/.

Business Insider. "Inside Alinea — and How Its Star Chef Comes up with the Menu." YouTube, October 7, 2017. https://www.youtube.com/watch?v=j8T5Lo2n4-Q.

Catmull, Ed. "How Pixar Fosters Collective Creativity." Harvard Business Review, September 2008. https://hbr.org/2008/09/how-pixar-fosters-collective-creativity.

Chef's Table. Film. Netflix, 2019.

Da Vinci, Leonardo. *Leonardo's Notebooks: Writing and Art of the Great Master*. Edited by H. Anna Suh. Black Dog & Leventhal, 2013.

———. *Trattato Della Pittura*. Paris, France, 1651.

Foodpairing. "Flavor Bouncing or Foodpairing Explained by Grant Achatz of Alinea Restaurant." YouTube, November 19, 2015. https://www.youtube.com/watch?v=9303-2ygFkA&t=2s.

Graduate, Stanford. "Ed Catmull, Pixar: Keep Your Crises Small." YouTube, July 28, 2009. https://www.youtube.com/watch?v=k2h2lvhzMDc.

Hart, Hugh. "Lessons in Creating Surprise from Pioneering Chef Grant Achatz." Fast Company, October 30, 2013. https://www.fastcompany.com/3020591/lessons-in-creating-surprise-from-pioneering-chef-grant-achatz.

SOURCE NOTES

HK Choi, Mary. "The Rise of Christina Tosi's Milk Bar Empire." *Eater*, September 5, 2017. https://www.eater.com/2017/9/5/16213430/christina-tosi-profile-milk-bar.

King, Stephen. *On Writing: A Memoir of the Craft.* 2000. Reprint, London: Hodder, 2012.

Leaf, Clifton. "Pixar's Ed Catmull: If Something Works, You Shouldn't Do It Again." *Fortune*, July 14, 2015. https://fortune.com/2015/07/14/pixar-catmull-disney-animation/.

MasterClass, and Aaron Sorkin. "Aaron Sorkin Teaches Screenwriting." Video Series. *MasterClass*, n.d. https://www.masterclass.com/classes/aaron-sorkin-teaches-screenwriting.

Max, D.T. "A Chef Battles for His Sense of Taste." *The New Yorker*, May 5, 2008. https://www.newyorker.com/magazine/2008/05/12/a-man-of-taste.

McCulley, Carolyn. "Sonic Illusions." Twenty Thousand Hertz, June 2019. https://www.20k.org/episodes/sonicillusions.

McLaughlin, Katy. "Finding Poetry in Food (and Vice Versa)." *Wall Street Journal*, July 21, 2012, sec. Life and Style. https://www.wsj.com/articles/SB10000872396390444330904577535033879275676.

Michalko, Michael. "Creative Thinking and Leonardo Da Vinci." Thinkjarcollective. com, 2019. https://thinkjarcollective.com/articles/creative-thinking-leonardo-da-vinci/.

NME. "Taylor Swift – How I Wrote My Massive Hit 'Blank Space.'" YouTube, October 5, 2015. https://www.youtube.com/watch?v=8bYUDY4lmls.

Pacchioli, David. "Making Connections: Psychologist Explores the Neuroscience of Creativity | Penn State University." www.psu.edu, December 1, 2020. https://www.psu.edu/news/research/story/making-connections-psychologist-explores-neuroscience-creativity/.

Pompliano, Polina. "The Profile Dossier: Ed Catmull, Pixar's Creative Genius." theprofile.substack.com, May 5, 2021. https://theprofile.substack.com/p/the-profile-dossier-ed-catmull-pixars.

———. "The Profile Dossier: Grant Achatz, America's Most Creative Chef Playing Mind Games." theprofile.substack.com, September 9, 2020. https://theprofile.substack.com/p/the-profile-grant-achatz-americas?s=w.

Schnitzler, Nicole. "What I've Learned: Grant Achatz." *Esquire*, June 19, 2015. https://www.esquire.com/food-drink/food/a35818/what-ive-learned-grant-achatz/.

Snyder, Chris. "Inside the Best Restaurant in America — and How Its Star Chef Comes up with Elaborate 19-Course Tasting Menus." Business Insider, September 15, 2017. https://www.businessinsider.com/how-best-restaurant-america-alinea-creates-menu-2017-9.

Stillman, Jessica. "Why the Best Ideas Fail the Elevator Test, according to Pixar's Ed Catmull." Inc.com, May 11, 2021. https://www.inc.com/jessica-stillman/why-best-ideas-fail-elevator-test-according-to-pixars-ed-catmull.html.

Studio E. "Life Lessons from Milk Bar Founder, Christina Tosi." Studio/E, August 11, 2020. https://yourstudioe.com/blog/christina-tosi-life-lessons/.

Tanaka, Jennifer. "Burned: The Story of Grant Achatz's Cancer Recovery." Chicago Magazine, June 5, 2008. https://www.chicagomag.com/Chicago-Magazine/June-2008/Burned/.

University, Carnegie Mellon. "Press Release: Carnegie Mellon Brain Imaging Research Shows How Unconscious Processing Improves Decision-Making - News - Carnegie Mellon University." www.cmu.edu, February 13, 2013. https://www.cmu.edu/news/stories/archives/2013/february/feb13_unconsciousthought.html.

Urban, Tim. "The Elon Musk Post Series." Wait But Why, March 28, 2017. https://waitbutwhy.com/2017/03/elon-musk-post-series.html.

Vettel, Phil. "Alinea Named World's Best Restaurant by Elite Traveler." Chicago Tribune, April 18, 2018. https://www.chicagotribune.com/dining/ct-food-alinea-number-one-0418-story.html.

Vox. "The Sound Illusion That Makes Dunkirk so Intense." YouTube, July 26, 2017. https://www.youtube.com/watch?v=LVWTQcZbLgY.

WIRED Staff. "Steve Jobs: The next Insanely Great Thing." WIRED. WIRED, February 1996. https://www.wired.com/1996/02/jobs-2/.

CHAPTER 2

Abagnale, Frank W, and Barrett Whitener. Catch Me If You Can. Ashland, Or: Blackstone Audiobooks, 2002.

Davidgoggins.com. "ABOUT | David Goggins," 2015. https://davidgoggins.com/about/.

Agnew, Danny. "A Former Navy SEAL Schools Us on the Art of Resilience." InsideHook. Accessed August 10, 2022. https://www.insidehook.com/feature/advice/a-former-navy-seal-schools-us-on-the-art-of-resilience.

Babb, Kent. "Kobe Bryant, Revising His Own History." Washington Post, November 14, 2018. https://www.washingtonpost.com/graphics/2018/sports/kobe-bryant-hollywood-revisionist/.

Barker, Sarah. "Ultrarunner Courtney Dauwalter Explains Why She Runs through Blindness and Hallucinations." Deadspin, June 13, 2018. https://deadspin.com/ultrarunner-courtney-dauwalter-explains-why-she-runs-th-1826672881.

SOURCE NOTES

BigThink. "From 300lbs to a Navy SEAL: How to Gain Control of Your Mind and Life." Big Think. Accessed August 10, 2022. https://bigthink.com/videos/david-goggins-to-win-in-life-win-the-war-in-your-mind-navy-seal/.

Bilyeu, Tom. "Become a Savage & Live on Your Own Terms | David Goggins on Impact Theory." YouTube, December 11, 2018. https://www.youtube.com/watch?v=dIM7E8e9JKY.

Boone, Amelia. "Big's Backyard Ultra: Just What I Needed." Race Ipsa Loquitur, October 28, 2019. http://www.ameliabooneracing.com/blog/sport/bigsbackyardultra/.

Bourn, Chris. "Why People like Trump Refer to Themselves in the Third Person." MEL Magazine, April 27, 2018. https://melmagazine.com/en-us/story/the-psychology-of-referring-to-yourself-in-the-third-person.

Caldwell, Tommy. *PUSH: A Climber's Journey of Endurance, Risk, and Going beyond Limits*. Penguin Publishing Group, 2018.

Clear, James. "Identity-Based Habits: How to Actually Stick to Your Goals This Year." James Clear, December 31, 2012. https://jamesclear.com/identity-based-habits.

Crosley, Hillary. "Beyonce Says She 'Killed' Sasha Fierce." MTV, February 26, 2010. https://www.mtv.com/news/13z2bh/beyonce-says-she-killed-sasha-fierce.

Eger, Edith Eva. *The Choice*. London: Rider, 2018.

Elkins, Kathleen. "Retired Navy SEAL: This Mentality 'Rubs Everybody the Wrong Way' but It Led to My Success." CNBC, April 4, 2019. https://www.cnbc.com/2019/04/04/ex-navy-seal-david-goggins-this-mentality-led-to-my-success.html.

Goggins, David, and Lioncrest Publishing. *Can't Hurt Me: Master Your Mind and Defy the Odds*. Miejsce Nieznane: Lioncrest Publishing, Druk, 2019.

Google Zeitgeist. "'I Want to Find the Impossible' | Tommy Caldwell & Lynn Hill | Google Zeitgeist." YouTube, October 20, 2015. https://www.youtube.com/watch?v=kboFNeB_n08.

Hinton, Anthony Ray. "I Spent 28 Years on Death Row." *The Guardian*, October 21, 2016. https://www.theguardian.com/lifeandstyle/2016/oct/21/28-years-on-death-row.

Howes, Lewis. "Master Your Mind and Defy the Odds with David Goggins." Lewis Howes, November 5, 2018. https://lewishowes.com/podcast/master-your-mind-and-defy-the-odds-with-david-goggins/.

Johnson, Caitlin. "Beyoncé on Love, Depression and Reality." Cbsnews.com, December 13, 2006. https://www.cbsnews.com/news/beyonce-on-love-depression-and-reality/.

Kobe Bryant's Muse. Streamed. Showtime, 2015.

Mann, Don, and Ralph Pezzullo. *Inside Seal Team Six: My Life and Missions with America's Elite Warriors.* New York: Back Bay Books, 2012.

Parrish, Shane. "Amelia Boone: Learning How to Suffer with the Queen of Pain." Farnam Street. Accessed August 10, 2022. https://fs.blog/knowledge-project-podcast/amelia-boone/.

Polina, Marinova. "We Decoded Anthony Scaramucci's Profane Speaking Style. Here's What We Learned." Fortune, July 31, 2017. https://fortune.com/2017/07/31/anthony-scaramucci-comments-decoded/.

Pompliano, Polina. "7 Mentally Tough People on the Tactics They Use to Build Resilience." theprofile.substack.com, February 23, 2021. https://theprofile.substack.com/p/mental-toughness.

———. "Four-Time Obstacle Race Champion Amelia Boone on Mastering the Art of Suffering." theprofile.substack.com, April 6, 2021. https://theprofile.substack.com/p/amelia-boone.

———. "The Profile Dossier: Anthony Ray Hinton, the Innocent Man on Death Row." The Profile, June 24, 2020. https://theprofile.substack.com/p/the-profile-dossier-anthony-ray-hinton.

———. "The Profile Dossier: Cheryl Strayed, the Wanderer Who Found Peace." theprofile.substack.com, September 30, 2020. https://theprofile.substack.com/p/the-profile-dossier-cheryl-strayed.

———. "Why the World's Most Confident People Create Alter Egos." theprofile.substack.com, August 27, 2020. https://theprofile.substack.com/p/why-the-worlds-most-confident-people?s=w.

PowerfulJRE. "Joe Rogan Experience #1080 - David Goggins." YouTube, February 19, 2018. https://www.youtube.com/watch?v=5tSTk1083VY.

Roberts, LaVonne. "After ALS Struck, He Became the World's Most Advanced Cyborg." Input, December 29, 2021. https://www.inputmag.com/culture/dr-peter-scott-morgan-als-ai-cyborg.

Roll, Rich. "Navy SEAL David Goggins Is the Toughest Athlete on Earth -- Thoughts on Mindset, the 40% Rule & Why Purpose Always Trumps Motivation." Rich Roll, January 2, 2017. https://www.richroll.com/podcast/david-goggins/.

Rooney, Austin. "The Toughest Man Alive." Navy All Hands, November 27, 2018. https://allhands.navy.mil/Stories/Display-Story/Article/1840612/the-toughest-man-alive/.

Segalov, Michael. "'I Choose to Thrive': The Man Fighting Motor Neurone Disease with Cyborg Technology." *The Guardian*, August 16, 2020. https://www.theguardian.com/society/2020/aug/16/i-choose-to-thrive-the-man-fighting-motor-neurone-disease-with-cyborg-technology.

Strayed, Cheryl. *Wild: From Lost to Found on the Pacific Crest Trail.* New York: Alfred A. Knopf, 2012.

SUUNTORUN. "Courtney Dauwalter and Her Pursuit of Mind Power." Suunto, April 20, 2020. https://www.suunto.com/en-us/sports/News-Articles-container-page/courtney-dauwalter-and-her-pursuit-of-mind-power/.

TEDx Talks. "What Are You up Against? | Tommy Caldwell | TEDxKC." YouTube, September 15, 2015. https://www.youtube.com/watch?v=PnMs_qLwaes.

The Jordan Harbinger Show. "Tommy Caldwell | the Push for the Path Upwards." Jordan Harbinger, September 24, 2019. https://www.jordanharbinger.com/tommy-caldwell-the-push-for-the-path-upwards/.

Trail Runner Magazine. "How Courtney Dauwalter Won the Moab 240 Outright." Trail Runner Magazine, October 19, 2017. https://www.trailrunnermag.com/people/news-people/courtney-dauwalter-wins-moab-240/.

CHAPTER 3

Benedictus, Luke, Jeremy Macvean, and Andrew Mcutchen. *The Father Hood: Inspiration for the New Dad Generation.* Sydney: Murdoch Books, An Imprint Of Allen & Unwin, 2019.

Benson, Kyle. "The Magic Relationship Ratio, according to Science." The Gottman Institute, October 4, 2017. https://www.gottman.com/blog/the-magic-relationship-ratio-according-science/.

Brittle, Zach. "R Is for Repair." The Gottman Institute, September 3, 2014. https://www.gottman.com/blog/r-is-for-repair/.

Coates, Tyler. "For Esther Perel, Romance and Power Are Intertwined." www.yahoo.com, October 29, 2018. https://www.yahoo.com/now/esther-perel-romance-power-intertwined-040000445.html.

Dmy, Phil. "[Complete] Charlie Munger USC Law Commencement Speech - May 2007." YouTube, May 2007. https://www.youtube.com/watch?v=jY1eNlL6NKs.

Farnam Street. "The Munger Operating System: A Life That Works." Farnam Street, April 13, 2016. https://fs.blog/munger-operating-system/.

Greater Good Science Center. "John Gottman: How to Build Trust." YouTube, October 28, 2011. https://www.youtube.com/watch?v=rgWnadSi91s.

John Mordechai Gottman, and Nan Silver. *Why Marriages Succeed or Fail: And How You Can Make Yours Last.* London: Bloomsbury Publishing, 2007.

Kornbluth, Jesse. "Esther Perel: Whether You're Experiencing a Second Honeymoon or Married Bed Death, She Can Help." headbutler.com, February 16, 2021. https://

headbutler.com/reviews/esther-perel-sex-has-nothing-to-do-with-where-you-put-your-hand-its-about-where-you-can-take-me-not-what-you-can-do-to-me/.

Lisitsa, Ellie. "An Introduction to Emotional Bids and Trust." The Gottman Institute, September 1, 2012. https://www.gottman.com/blog/an-introduction-to-emotional-bids-and-trust/.

Marie Claire. "The New American Couple." Marie Claire Magazine, March 20, 2011. https://www.marieclaire.com/sex-love/advice/a5915/new-american-couple/.

Masters of Scale. "How to Build Trust Fast." Masters of Scale, February 20, 2019. https://mastersofscale.com/daniel-ek-how-to-build-trust-fast/.

Meyer, Danny. Setting the Table: The Transforming Power of Hospitality in Business. New York: Harper, 2008.

———. "Play Long-Term Games with Long-Term People." Naval, March 19, 2019. https://nav.al/long-term.

Perel, Esther, and Mary Alice Miller. "From Esther Perel's Blog - Six Essential Practices to Improve Listening Skills in Relationships." www.estherperel.com, n.d. https://www.estherperel.com/blog/six-essential-practices-to-improve-listening-skills-in-relationships.

Pompliano, Polina. "100 Couples Share Their Secrets to a Successful Relationship." theprofile.substack.com, July 16, 2020. https://theprofile.substack.com/p/100-couples-share-their-secrets-to?s=r.

———. "Danny Meyer on Leading in Crisis, Developing an Appetite for Risk, and Building a Hospitality Empire." theprofile.substack.com, November 4, 2021. https://theprofile.substack.com/p/danny-meyer-interview?s=w.

Ravikant, Naval. "Compounding Relationships Make Life Easier." Naval, July 19, 2019. https://nav.al/relationships.

Raz, Guy. "Esther Perel: How Can Couples Rebuild Trust after an Affair?" NPR.org, May 15, 2015. https://www.npr.org/transcripts/406455947.

TedxTalks. "The Science of Love | John Gottman | TEDxVeniceBeach." YouTube, October 2, 2018. https://www.youtube.com/watch?v=-uazFBCDvVw.

The Gottman Institute. "Love Lab." The Gottman Institute, 2015. https://www.gottman.com/love-lab/.

———. "Overview - Research | Tthe Gottman Institute." The Gottman Institute, 2015. https://www.gottman.com/about/research/.

———. "What Distinguishes the 'Masters' of Relationships from the 'Disasters?' | Dr. John Gottman." YouTube, April 10, 2015. https://www.youtube.com/watch?v=INo8RSgnviA.

The Knowledge Project. "Chris Voss: The Art of Letting Other People Have Your

Way [the Knowledge Project Ep. #27]." Farnam Street. Accessed August 15, 2022. https://fs.blog/knowledge-project-podcast/chris-voss/.

Underscore VC. "No-Nonsense | Featuring Tobi Lutke, Co-Founder & CEO of Shopify." Underscore VC, October 30, 2019. https://underscore.vc/blog/no-nonsense-featuring-tobi-lutke/.

Voss, Chris, and MasterClass. "Chris Voss Teaches the Art of Negotiation." MasterClass, n.d. https://www.masterclass.com/classes/chris-voss-teaches-the-art-of-negotiation.

CHAPTER 4

Lori Gottlieb. "About Lori Gottlieb, Psychotherapist and Award-Winning Author," n.d. https://lorigottlieb.com/about/.

Behind the Curtain. "How I Wrote the Social Network (Aaron Sorkin's Writing Process)." YouTube Video. YouTube, May 21, 2019. https://www.youtube.com/watch?v=PNarYM5t4TA.

Carr, David. *The Night of the Gun: A Reporter Investigates the Darkest Story of His Life, His Own.* New York: Simon & Schuster Paperbacks, 2009.

Columbia Journalism School. "Columbia Journalism School 2018 Graduation - Ira Glass." YouTube, 2018. https://www.youtube.com/watch?v=nVc1kZf8hRY&t=23s.

Du Maurier, Daphne. *Rebecca.* 1938. Reprint, HarperCollins, 2010.

Erik Anderson. "16th Final Draft Award Honorees: Aaron Sorkin, Steve McQueen, Sofia Coppola, Ramy Youssef and Radha Blank." AwardsWatch, November 18, 2020. https://awardswatch.com/16th-final-draft-award-honorees-aaron-sorkin-steve-mcqueen-sofia-coppola-ramy-youssef-and-radha-blank/.

Evans, Robert. *The Kid Stays in the Picture.* Pxok/June, 2009.

Ferriss, Tim. "Brandon Stanton – the Story of Humans of New York and 25M+ Fans (#321)." The Blog of Author Tim Ferriss, February 15, 2019. https://tim.blog/2018/06/18/brandon-stanton-humans-of-new-york/.

Glass, Ira. "Ira Glass's Commencement Speech at the Columbia Journalism School Graduation." This American Life, May 17, 2018. https://www.thisamericanlife.org/about/announcements/ira-glass-commencement-speech.

Gottlieb, Lori. "How Changing Your Story Can Change Your Life." *TED,* November 1, 2019. https://www.ted.com/talks/lori_gottlieb_how_changing_your_story_can_change_your_life.

———. *Maybe You Should Talk to Someone: A Therapist, Her Therapist, and Our Lives Revealed.* S.L.: Mariner Books, 2020.

Hawkins, Paula. *The Girl on the Train.* London: Transworld Publishers Ltd, 2015.

Hello Monday. "Hello Monday with Jessi Hempel: Boosting Your Psychological Immune System with Lori Gottlieb on Apple Podcasts." Apple Podcasts. Accessed August 15, 2022. https://podcasts.apple.com/us/podcast/boosting-your-psychological-immune-system-lori-gottlieb/id1453893304?i=1000474938999.

Lewis, Malcolm. "AirBnB Pitch Deck." SlideShare, March 12, 2015. https://www.slideshare.net/PitchDeckCoach/airbnb-first-pitch-deck-editable.

Longform. "Longform Podcast #64: Gay Talese · Longform." Longform, October 13, 2013. https://longform.org/posts/longform-podcast-64-gay-talese.

NJ.com, Mark Di Ionno | Advance Local Media. "Lessons on Writing -- and Life -- from Gay Talese | Di Ionno." nj, February 16, 2017. https://www.nj.com/news/2017/02/lessons_on_writing_--_and_life_--_from_gay_talese.html

Palahniuk, Chuck. Fight Club. 1996. Reprint, New York: W.W. Norton & Company, 2018.

Poe, Edgar Allan. The Tell-Tale Heart. 1843. Reprint, Edina, Minn.: Magic Wagon, 2010.

Pompliano, Polina. "Inside the Mind of 'Humans of New York' Creator Brandon Stanton." theprofile.substack.com, October 20, 2020. https://theprofile.substack.com/p/inside-the-mind-of-humans-of-new?s=w.

———. "The Profile Dossier: Aaron Sorkin, the Mastermind behind America's Favorite Films." theprofile.substack.com, November 11, 2020. https://theprofile.substack.com/p/the-profile-dossier-aaron-sorkin.

———. "The Profile Dossier: Al Pacino, Hollywood's Favorite Gangster." theprofile.substack.com, May 26, 2021. https://theprofile.substack.com/p/al-pacino.

———. "The Profile Dossier: Fred Rogers, the Nicest Man in the Neighborhood." theprofile.substack.com, June 10, 2020. https://theprofile.substack.com/p/the-profile-dossier-fred-rogers-the.

———. "The Profile Dossier: Ira Glass, the King of Storytelling." theprofile.substack.com, April 20, 2020. https://theprofile.substack.com/p/ira-glass-the-king-of-storytelling.

———. "The Profile Dossier: Lin-Manuel Miranda, the King of Broadway." theprofile.substack.com, October 28, 2020. https://theprofile.substack.com/p/lin-manuel-miranda.

———. "The Profile Dossier: Melanie Perkins, the Billionaire Founder of the World's Most Valuable Software Startup." theprofile.substack.com, February 16, 2022. https://theprofile.substack.com/p/melanie-perkins-the-billionaire-founder.

Rogers, Fred. Wisdom from the World according to Mister Rogers. Peter Pauper Press, 2006.

Steigerwald, Shauna. "Nine Lessons from Jim Koch of Sam Adams." The Enquirer,

February 4, 2016. https://www.cincinnati.com/story/entertainment/2016/02/04/nine-lessons-jim-koch-sam-adams/79750656/.

Talese, Gay. "Frank Sinatra Has a Cold." *Esquire*, May 14, 2016. https://www.esquire.com/news-politics/a638/frank-sinatra-has-a-cold-gay-talese/.

———. "Mr. Bad News | Esquire | February 1966." Esquire | The Complete Archive, February 1, 1966. https://classic.esquire.com/article/1966/2/1/mr-bad-news.

The Editors at CJR. "Q&A: Ira Glass on Structuring Stories, Asking Hard Questions." Columbia Journalism Review, June 22, 2017. https://www.cjr.org/special_report/qa-ira-glass-turnaround-npr-jesse-thorn-tal.php.

This American Life. "472: Our Friend David." This American Life, December 14, 2017. https://www.thisamericanlife.org/472/transcript.

University of Pennsylvania. "Penn's 2016 Commencement Ceremony-Commencement Speaker Lin-Manuel Miranda." YouTube, May 16, 2016. https://www.youtube.com/watch?v=ewHcsFlolz4.

CHAPTER 5

Bowman, Bob. *Golden Rules: 10 Steps to World-Class Excellence in Your Life and Work.* St. Martin's Press, 2018.

Brennan, Thomas James. "Inside the Painstaking Recovery Process of a Medal of Honor Marine." Vanity Fair, November 11, 2016. https://www.vanityfair.com/news/2016/11/medal-of-honor-marine-recovery.

Bryant, Adam. "Tobi Lütke of Shopify: Powering a Team with a 'Trust Battery.'" *The New York Times*, April 22, 2016. https://www.nytimes.com/2016/04/24/business/tobi-lutke-of-shopify-powering-a-team-with-a-trust-battery.html.

Carpenter, Kyle. *You Are Worth It: Building a Life Worth Fighting For.* William Morrow, 2020.

Columbia Magazine. "Learn Africa, Says Nobel Laureate Leymah Gbowee." Columbia Magazine, 2013. https://magazine.columbia.edu/article/learn-africa-says-nobel-laureate-leymah-gbowee.

Feloni, Richard. "How Aetna's Former CEO Found a Blueprint for Leadership in an Ancient Taoist Text." Business Insider, March 15, 2019. https://www.businessinsider.com/former-aetna-ceo-mark-bertolinis-taoist-leadership-lesson-2019-3?utm_source=pocket_mylist.

Jocko Podcast. "Jocko Podcast 207 with Kyle Carpenter, Medal of Honor Recipient. Live a Life Worth Fighting For." YouTube, December 12, 2019. https://www.youtube.com/watch?v=S1ctMlVSbro.

Kavanaugh, Nadine. "Marc Lore's Secret to Serial Entrepreneurship?" Wharton Magazine, April 13, 2015. https://magazine.wharton.upenn.edu/digital/marc-lores-secret-to-serial-entrepreneurship/.

Kawasaki, Guy. "Dr. Robert Cialdini: The Psychology Powering Influence and Persuasion." Guy Kawasaki, January 15, 2020. https://guykawasaki.com/dr-robert-cialdini-the-godfather-of-influence/.

Krishnan, Sriram. "The Observer Effect – Daniel Ek." www.theobservereffect.org, n.d. https://www.theobservereffect.org/daniel.html.

———. "The Observer Effect – Tobi Lütke." www.theobservereffect.org, n.d. https://www.theobservereffect.org/tobi.html.

BlogTalkRadio. "Kyle Carpenter Medal of Honor Recipient Discusses Life Lessons." Accessed August 16, 2022. https://www.blogtalkradio.com/veterans_radio/2019/10/15/kyle-carpenter-medal-of-honor-recipient-discusses-life-lessons.

Laozi, and James Legge. The Tao Te Ching. Simon & Brown, 2018.

Martell, Dan. "The Future of Retail 'Arming the Rebels!' with Tobi Lütke @ Shopify.com - Escape Velocity Show #16." YouTube, December 5, 2019. https://www.youtube.com/watch?v=-PZ0uDwpIYQ.

MasterClass. "Sara Blakely Teaches Self-Made Entrepreneurship." MasterClass, n.d. https://www.masterclass.com/classes/sara-blakely-teaches-self-made-entrepreneurship.

Masters of Scale. "Masters of Scale: Rapid Response: Danny Meyer on the Wrenching Decision to Do Layoffs on Apple Podcasts." Apple Podcasts. Accessed August 16, 2022. https://podcasts.apple.com/us/podcast/rapid-response-danny-meyer-on-the-wrenching-decision/id1227971746?i=1000469398313.

Mead, Rebecca. "The Prince of Solomeo." The New Yorker, March 29, 2010. https://www.newyorker.com/magazine/2010/03/29/the-prince-of-solomeo.

Meyer, Danny. Setting the Table: The Transforming Power of Hospitality in Business. New York: Harper, 2008.

New York Times Events. "The Science of Influence." YouTube, March 7, 2017. https://www.youtube.com/watch?v=IQoiEKRyztc.

Pompliano, Polina. "Bridgewater Co-CEO Mark Bertolini on the Value of 'Radical Transparency' and Taking over from Ray Dalio." theprofile.substack.com, August 17, 2022. https://theprofile.substack.com/p/mark-bertolini-interview.

———. "The Profile Dossier: Bernard Arnault, the World's Richest Man." theprofile.substack.com, August 11, 2021. https://theprofile.substack.com/p/bernard-arnault#details.

———. "The Profile Dossier: Bob Bowman, the Coach Who Produces Champions."

theprofile.substack.com, October 14, 2020. https://theprofile.substack.com/p/the-profile-dossier-bob-bowman-the.

———. "The Profile Dossier: Brunello Cucinelli, the Philosopher King of Cashmere." theprofile.substack.com, February 24, 2021. https://theprofile.substack.com/p/brunello-cucinelli.

———. "The Profile Dossier: Daniel Ek, the No-Nonsense Founder Who Built a Creative Empire." theprofile.substack.com, December 16, 2020. https://theprofile.substack.com/p/the-profile-dossier-daniel-ek-the.

———. "The Profile Dossier: Danny Meyer, the King of Hospitality." theprofile.substack.com, September 15, 2021. https://theprofile.substack.com/p/the-profile-dossier-danny-meyer-the.

———. "The Profile Dossier: Esther Wojcicki, the Educator Who Raised Entrepreneurial Children." theprofile.substack.com, May 19, 2021. https://theprofile.substack.com/p/the-profile-dossier-esther-wojcicki.

———. "The Profile Dossier: Kyle Carpenter, the Fearless Warrior Who Came Back from the Dead." theprofile.substack.com, August 5, 2020. https://theprofile.substack.com/p/the-profile-dossier-kyle-carpenter.

———. "The Profile Dossier: Leymah Gbowee, the Peace Activist Who Ended a 14-Year Civil War." theprofile.substack.com, December 8, 2021. https://theprofile.substack.com/p/leymah-gbowee.

———. "The Profile Dossier: Marc Lore, the Serial Entrepreneur Building Billion-Dollar Companies." theprofile.substack.com, May 11, 2022. https://theprofile.substack.com/p/marc-lore?s=w.

———. "The Profile Dossier: Melanie Perkins, the Billionaire Founder of the World's Most Valuable Software Startup." theprofile.substack.com, February 16, 2022. https://theprofile.substack.com/p/melanie-perkins-the-billionaire-founder.

———. "The Profile Dossier: Robert Cialdini, the Master of Persuasion." theprofile.substack.com, June 30, 2021. https://theprofile.substack.com/p/robert-cialdini.

———. "The Profile Dossier: Sara Blakely, the Self-Made Billionaire." theprofile.substack.com, May 20, 2020. https://theprofile.substack.com/p/the-profile-dossier-sara-blakely.

———. "The Profile Dossier: Tobi Lütke, the Founder Who Believes in Arming the Rebels." theprofile.substack.com, October 27, 2021. https://theprofile.substack.com/p/tobi-lutke.

Safian, Robert. "Exclusive: Spotify CEO Daniel Ek on Apple, Facebook, Netflix—and the Future." Fast Company, August 7, 2018. https://www.fastcompany.com/90213545/exclusive-spotify-ceo-daniel-ek-on-apple-facebook-netflix-and-the-future-of-music.

South Carolina Gamecocks. "Cpl. Kyle Carpenter Speaks to Gamecock Men's

Soccer." YouTube, June 19, 2014. https://www.youtube.com/watch?v=-cW4XxOP1GM&feature=youtu.be.

Underscore VC. "No-Nonsense | Featuring Tobi Lutke, Co-Founder & CEO of Shopify." Underscore VC, October 30, 2019. https://underscore.vc/blog/no-nonsense-featuring-tobi-lutke/.

Wetlaufer, Suzy. "The Perfect Paradox of Star Brands: An Interview with Bernard Arnault of LVMH." Harvard Business Review, October 1, 2001. https://hbr.org/2001/10/the-perfect-paradox-of-star-brands-an-interview-with-bernard-arnault-of-lvmh.

Wojcicki, Esther. *How to Raise Successful People: Simple Lessons for Radical Results.* Boston: Houghton Mifflin Harcourt, 2019.

Good Life Project. "You Are Worth It | Kyle Carpenter." Accessed August 16, 2022. https://www.goodlifeproject.com/podcast/kyle-carpenter/.

Zeng, Jianji, and Guangyi Xu. "How Servant Leadership Motivates Innovative Behavior: A Moderated Mediation Model." *International Journal of Environmental Research and Public Health* 17, no. 13 (July 2, 2020): 4753. https://doi.org/10.3390/ijerph17134753.

Zipkin, Nina. "She Was Told 'No' 100 Times. Now This 31-Year-Old Female Founder Runs a $1 Billion Business." Entrepreneur, June 12, 2019. https://www.entrepreneur.com/article/310482.

CHAPTER 6

52 Insights. "Garrett McNamara | On the Shoulders of Giants." 52 Insights, December 29, 2016. https://www.52-insights.com/garrett-mcnamara-on-the-shoulders-of-giants-interview-surfing-wave/.

60 Minutes. "Russian Free Diver Alexey Molchanov: The 60 Minutes Interview." www.cbsnews.com, September 26, 2021. https://www.cbsnews.com/video/free-diving-alexey-molchanov-60-minutes-video-2021-09-26/#x.

Aprendemos Juntos 2030. "V.O. Complete. A Spaceman's Guide to Life on Earth. Chris Hadfield, Astronaut." YouTube, January 26, 2019. https://www.youtube.com/watch?v=tuicma_u9SA.

Averill, Graham. "Even a Heart Attack Can't Slow 56-Year-Old Conrad Anker Down." Outside Online, April 14, 2019. https://www.outsideonline.com/health/training-performance/conrad-anker-climbing-heart-attack/.

Corrigan, Kevin. "Alex Lowe and David Bridges' Bodies Found on Shishapangma." Climbing, May 1, 2016. https://www.climbing.com/news/alex-lowe-and-david-bridgess-bodies-found-on-shishapangma/.

Edmondson, Laurence. "Lewis Hamilton Is Building a 'Masterpiece.'" ESPN. com, November 4, 2019. https://www.espn.com/f1/story/_/id/28007004/lewis-hamilton-building-masterpiece.

Katy Vine. "The Astronaut Who Might Actually Get Us to Mars." Texas Monthly, 23 Jan. 2018, www.texasmonthly.com/articles/the-astronaut-who-might-actually-get-us-to-mars/.

Fallows, James. "The Steve Jobs of Beer." The Atlantic, October 15, 2014. https://www.theatlantic.com/magazine/archive/2014/11/the-steve-jobs-of-beer/380790/.

Formula 1. "Discover How Lewis Hamilton Went from 22-Year-Old Rookie to Six-Time Champion in Aramco Presents: Rise of the Rookie | Formula 1®." www.formula1.com, August 20, 2020. https://www.formula1.com/en/latest/article.discover-how-hamilton-went-from-22-year-old-rookie-to-six-time-champ-in-aramco-presents.1pfo94Ii7zfoWXXmpjGloz.html.

Gill, Pete. "Lewis Hamilton Joins Mercedes for 2013: The Potential Winners and Losers." Sky Sports, April 10, 2012. https://www.skysports.com/f1/news/22058/8129689/lewis-hamilton-joins-mercedes-for-2013-the-potential-winners-and-losers.

Great Big Story. "Building the Engine That Will Take Us to Mars." YouTube, December 17, 2019. https://www.youtube.com/watch?v=jiBVs9ZwA-Q.

Hadfield, Chris. An Astronaut's Guide to Life on Earth. Toronto: Vintage Canada, 2015.

HBO. "100 Foot Wave | Official Website for the HBO Series | HBO.com." www.hbo.com, 2022. https://www.hbo.com/100-foot-wave.

Housel, Morgan. "The Three Sides of Risk." Collaborative Fund, August 8, 2020. https://www.collaborativefund.com/blog/the-three-sides-of-risk/.

JFK Library. "Space Summit: Welcome, ISS Greeting, and Former NASA Astronaut Dr. Franklin Chang Diaz (2019)." YouTube, July 26, 2019. https://www.youtube.com/watch?v=bT-9zJ7BE1M.

jgoodman@al.com, Joseph Goodman |. "Rare Look into Alabama's Legendary Pregame Meetings Led by Nick Saban." al, December 30, 2015. https://www.al.com/sports/2015/12/a_rare_look_into_alabamas_lege.html.

Joffrion, Emily Fields. "4 Founders Share Their Secret for Overcoming Failure at How I Built This Summit." Forbes, October 29, 2019. https://www.forbes.com/sites/emilyjoffrion/2019/10/29/4-ceos-share-their-secret-for-overcoming-failure-at-how-i-built-this-summit/?sh=13ddf75f1ba2.

Luscombe, Belinda. "Life after Death." Time, 2017. https://time.com/sheryl-sandberg-option-b/.

Mcnamara, Garrett, and Karen Karbo. Hound of the Sea: Wild Man, Wild Waves, Wild Wisdom. New York: Harperwave, 2017.

Molchanovs Freediving. "Molchanovs Movement | Visualization Techniques with Alexey Molchanov | Molchanovs Freediving." YouTube, March 27, 2020. https://www.youtube.com/watch?v=6tK-6IbUcXI.

Mutrie, Tim. "Climbers Describe Deadly Avalanche." www.aspentimes.com, May 14, 2003. https://www.aspentimes.com/news/climbers-describe-deadly-avalanche/.

Netflix. "Watch 14 Peaks: Nothing Is Impossible | Netflix Official Site." www.netflix.com, 2021. https://www.netflix.com/title/81464765.

NPR. "Samuel Adams: Jim Koch." NPR.org, July 24, 2017. https://www.npr.org/2017/09/05/538347944/samuel-adams-jim-koch.

———. "Stacy's Pita Chips: Stacy Madison (2019)." NPR.org, August 9, 2021. https://www.npr.org/2021/08/04/1024913084/stacys-pita-chips-stacy-madison-2019.

NPR Fresh Air. "Astronaut Chris Hadfield Brings Lessons from Space down to Earth." NPR.org, October 30, 2013. https://www.npr.org/2013/10/30/241830872/astronaut-chris-hadfield-brings-lessons-from-space-down-to-earth.

Phounrath, Pepsi. "Special Session with Dr. Franklin Chang Díaz,." NASA, September 18, 2020. https://www.nasa.gov/image-feature/special-session-with-dr-franklin-chang-d-az-former-nasa-astronaut/.

Pompliano, Polina. "The Profile Dossier: Alexey Molchanov, the World's Most Daring Freediver." theprofile.substack.com, October 20, 2021. https://theprofile.substack.com/p/alexey-molchanov.

———. "The Profile Dossier: Chris Hadfield, the Astronaut Who Conquered Fear." theprofile.substack.com, June 3, 2020. https://theprofile.substack.com/p/the-profile-dossier-chris-hadfield.

———. "The Profile Dossier: Franklin Chang Díaz, the Astronaut Who Wants to Get Humans to Mars." theprofile.substack.com, January 5, 2022. https://theprofile.substack.com/p/franklin-chang-diaz.

———. "The Profile Dossier: Jim Koch, the Self-Made Beer Billionaire." theprofile.substack.com, December 9, 2020. https://theprofile.substack.com/p/the-profile-dossier-jim-koch-the.

———. "The Profile Dossier: Lewis Hamilton, the Driver Revolutionizing Formula 1." theprofile.substack.com, March 30, 2022. https://theprofile.substack.com/p/the-profile-dossier-lewis-hamilton.

———. "The Profile Dossier: Lynsey Addario, the War Photographer Capturing Our Collective Humanity." theprofile.substack.com, June 8, 2022. https://theprofile.substack.com/p/the-profile-dossier-lynsey-addario?s=w.

———. "The Profile Dossier: Matt Mullenweg, the CEO Shaping the Future of the Internet." theprofile.substack.com, March 2, 2022. https://theprofile.substack.com/p/the-profile-dossier-matt-mullenweg.

————. "The Profile Dossier: Nims Purja, the Mountaineer Who Summited the World's 14 'Death Zone' Peaks." theprofile.substack.com, December 15, 2021. https://theprofile.substack.com/p/nims-purja.

————. "The Profile Dossier: Stacy Madison, the Creator of a Pita Chip Empire." theprofile.substack.com, January 5, 2022. https://theprofile.substack.com/p/stacy-madison-pita-chips.

Religion of Sports. "Rise | Full Episode | Religion of Sports | Season 3." YouTube, March 11, 2019. https://www.youtube.com/watch?v=SwY2soxwQSE.

Roach, Joshua Robinson | Photography by Cass Bird for WSJ Magazine | Styling by Law. "Lewis Hamilton, Star Formula 1 Driver, Plans to Revolutionize the Sport." *Wall Street Journal*, October 27, 2021, sec. Magazine. https://www.wsj.com/articles/lewis-hamilton-f1-driver-revolutionize-sport-profile-11635332391.

Rogan, Joe. "Joe Rogan Experience #414 - Cmdr. Chris Hadfield." JRE Podcast, November 11, 2013. https://www.jrepodcast.com/episode/joe-rogan-experience-414-cmdr-chris-hadfield/.

Rosberg, Nico. "'Surfing the World Record Wave' ft. Garrett McNamara | Beyond Victory #6." YouTube, November 20, 2018. https://www.youtube.com/watch?v=cYtsISU6M1I.

Sampiero, Josh. "The Nims Purja Paradox." Red Bull, December 7, 2021. https://www.redbull.com/us-en/nims-purja-interview-dreams-mission-project-possible.

Schaffer, Grayson. "Alex Lowe's Body Found on Shishapangma." Outside Online, April 30, 2016. https://www.outsideonline.com/outdoor-adventure/climbing/alex-lowes-body-found-shishapangma/.

Seftel, Josh. "NOVA | ScienceNOW | Profile: Franklin Chang-Díaz: Rocket Scientist | PBS." www.pbs.org, October 2, 2008. https://www.pbs.org/wgbh/nova/sciencenow/0403/04-diaz-nf.html.

TED. "What I Learned from Going Blind in Space | Chris Hadfield." YouTube, March 19, 2014. https://www.youtube.com/watch?v=Zo62SoulqhA.

The Knowledge Project. "Matt Mullenweg: Collaboration Is Key [the Knowledge Project Ep. #100]." Farnam Street. Accessed August 17, 2022. https://fs.blog/knowledge-project-podcast/matt-mullenweg/.

Turl, Jeff. "Don't Fear Failure and Don't Quit, Chris Hadfield Tells City Leaders." BayToday.ca, February 9, 2018. https://www.baytoday.ca/local-news/dont-fear-failure-and-dont-quit-chris-hadfield-tells-city-leaders-829629.

TVIW. "1-1 Dr. Franklin Chang Diaz, Living and Working in Space, an Astronaut's Perspective." YouTube, March 9, 2019. https://www.youtube.com/watch?v=7gwk-zyqU5Y.

University of Utah. "Conrad Anker Commencement Address." YouTube, May 8, 2017. https://www.youtube.com/watch?v=f7yRNCtrXqY.

Vaughn, Mark. "Lewis Hamilton's Thoughts on Racing... At Age 13." Autoweek, November 16, 2020. https://www.autoweek.com/racing/formula-1/a34680637/lewis-hamilton-age-13/.

Zubrow, Keith. "Watch Free Diving Star Alexey Molchanov Capture a World Record." www.cbsnews.com, July 31, 2022. https://www.cbsnews.com/news/free-diving-alexey-molchanov-world-record-60-minutes-2022-07-31/.

CHAPTER 7

Barden, Jamie, Derek D. Rucker, Richard E. Petty, and Kimberly Rios. "Order of Actions Mitigates Hypocrisy Judgments for Ingroup More than Outgroup Members." *SAGE Publications*, August 2013.

Clear, James. "Why Facts Don't Change Minds." James Clear, September 11, 2018. https://jamesclear.com/why-facts-dont-change-minds.

Dennett, Daniel. "The Folly of Pretence | Daniel Dennett." *The Guardian*. The Guardian, February 22, 2017. https://www.theguardian.com/commentisfree/belief/2009/jul/16/daniel-dennett-belief-atheism.

Farnam Street. "The Munger Operating System: A Life That Works." Farnam Street, April 13, 2016. https://fs.blog/munger-operating-system/.

Galef, Julia. "Rationally Speaking Podcast on Apple Podcasts." Apple Podcasts. Accessed August 18, 2022. https://podcasts.apple.com/us/podcast/rationally-speaking-podcast/id351953012.

———. "How to Want to Change Your Mind." YouTube. Accessed August 18, 2022. https://www.youtube.com/watch?v=fLGokkgnRkc&t=104s.

———. "Why You Think You're Right, Even When You're Wrong." ideas.ted.com, March 9, 2017. https://ideas.ted.com/why-you-think-youre-right-even-when-youre-wrong/.

Gecewicz, Claire. "'New Age' Beliefs Common among Both Religious and Nonreligious Americans." Pew Research Center, October 2018. https://www.pewresearch.org/fact-tank/2018/10/01/new-age-beliefs-common-among-both-religious-and-nonreligious-americans/.

Graham, Paul. "How to Think for Yourself." www.paulgraham.com, November 2020. http://www.paulgraham.com/think.html.

———. "The Four Quadrants of Conformism." www.paulgraham.com, July 2020. http://www.paulgraham.com/conformism.html.

SOURCE NOTES

HBO. "The Vow NXIVM Documentary Series - Official Website." HBO, 2020. https://www.hbo.com/the-vow.

Kappier, Maija. "3 Years after Leaving a Cult, Sarah Edmondson Is Still Questioning Everything." HuffPost, January 24, 2021. https://www.huffpost.com/archive/ca/entry/sarah-edmondson-nxivm-leaving-cult_ca_5fce5168c5b6636e09273820.

Krucoff, Carol. "The 6 O'Clock Scholar." *Washington Post*, January 29, 1984. https://www.washingtonpost.com/archive/lifestyle/1984/01/29/the-6-oclock-scholar/eed58de4-2dcb-47d2-8947-b0817a18d8fe/.

Leonhardt, Megan. "All the Things You're Doing Wrong When You Travel, according to Anthony Bourdain." Money, March 12, 2018. https://money.com/anthony-bourdain-advice-great-travel/.

Lerma, Martin. "Anthony Bourdain's Final Travel Book Is Coming This Fall. Here's What We Know." sports.yahoo.com, January 15, 2020. https://sports.yahoo.com/anthony-bourdain-final-travel-book-203002264.html.

Marinova, Polina. "Blackstone CEO Steve Schwarzman on Hong Kong's Unrest, the Rise of Bitcoin, and Fundraising as an 'Out-of-Body Experience.'" Fortune, September 17, 2019. https://fortune.com/2019/09/17/blackstone-ceo-steve-schwarzman-on-hong-kongs-unrest-the-rise-of-bitcoin-and-fundraising-as-an-out-of-body-experience/.

MasterClass. "Neil DeGrasse Tyson Teaches Scientific Thinking and Communication." MasterClass, n.d. https://www.masterclass.com/classes/neil-degrasse-tyson-teaches-scientific-thinking-and-communication.

Meier, Barry. "Inside a Secretive Group Where Women Are Branded." *The New York Times*, October 17, 2017, sec. New York. https://www.nytimes.com/2017/10/17/nyregion/nxivm-women-branded-albany.html.

Pompliano, Polina. "The Profile Dossier: Annie Duke, the Master of Uncertainty." theprofile.substack.com, March 25, 2020. https://theprofile.substack.com/p/the-profile-dossier-annie-duke-the.

———. "The Profile Dossier: Anthony Bourdain, the World's Most Beloved Chef." theprofile.substack.com, November 25, 2020. https://theprofile.substack.com/p/anthony-bourdain.

———. "The Profile Dossier: Julia Galef, the Rational Thinker Helping Us Update Our Beliefs." theprofile.substack.com, September 1, 2021. https://theprofile.substack.com/p/julia-galef.

———. "The Profile Dossier: Stephen Hawking, the Explorer of the Universe." theprofile.substack.com, February 17, 2021. https://theprofile.substack.com/p/stephen-hawking.

Storr, Will. "We All Play the Status Game, but Who Are the Real Winners?" *The*

Guardian, August 29, 2021. https://www.theguardian.com/society/2021/aug/29/we-all-play-the-status-game-but-who-are-the-real-winners.

Talks at Google. "Thinking in Bets | Annie Duke | Talks at Google." YouTube. Accessed August 18, 2022. https://www.youtube.com/watch?v=uYNsSeYjkp4.

The Ezra Klein Show. "Transcript: Julia Galef Interviews Philip Tetlock for 'the Ezra Klein Show.'" *The New York Times*, December 3, 2021, sec. Podcasts. https://www.nytimes.com/2021/12/03/podcasts/transcript-ezra-klein-podcast-philip-tetlock.html.

Tyson, Neil deGrasse. "Https://Twitter.com/Neiltyson/Status/1241107463803461636." Twitter, March 20, 2020. https://twitter.com/neiltyson/status/1241107463803461636?lang=en.

Weiss, Bari. "Honestly with Bari Weiss: How 'Luxury Beliefs' Hurt the Rest of Us on Apple Podcasts." Apple Podcasts. Accessed August 18, 2022. https://podcasts.apple.com/us/podcast/how-luxury-beliefs-hurt-the-rest-of-us/id1570872415?i=1000540733255.

CHAPTER 8

Adams, Tim. "John Cacioppo: 'Loneliness Is like an Iceberg – It Goes Deeper than We Can See.'" *The Guardian*, January 25, 2019. https://www.theguardian.com/science/2016/feb/28/loneliness-is-like-an-iceberg-john-cacioppo-social-neuroscience-interview.

Baiocchi, Stephanie. "Audience vs. Community: What's the Difference for Your Brand?" www.impactplus.com, August 14, 2019. https://www.impactplus.com/blog/audience-vs.-community-whats-the-difference-for-your-brand#:~:text=Author%20Chris%20Brogan%20once%20said.

BBC America. "Taylor Swift's Fans ★Die★ at 1989 Secret Listening Parties - the Graham Norton Show on BBC America." YouTube. Accessed July 19, 2021. https://www.youtube.com/watch?v=kGVg6gjBJ2w.

Brodesser-Akner, Taffy. "What Happened to Val Kilmer? He's Just Starting to Figure It Out." *The New York Times*, May 6, 2020. https://www.nytimes.com/2020/05/06/magazine/val-kilmer.html.

Fukada, Shiho. "Bloomberg - Are You a Robot?" Bloomberg.com, 2020. https://www.bloomberg.com/news/features/2018-03-16/japan-s-prisons-are-a-haven-for-elderly-women.

Gajanan, Mahita. "Taylor Swift Crashes Fan's Wedding." Vanity Fair, June 5, 2016. https://www.vanityfair.com/style/2016/06/taylor-swift-crashes-fan-wedding-for-surprise-performance.

SOURCE NOTES

Kramer, A. D. I., J. E. Guillory, and J. T. Hancock. "Experimental Evidence of Massive-Scale Emotional Contagion through Social Networks." *Proceedings of the National Academy of Sciences* 111, no. 24 (June 2, 2014): 8788–90. https://doi.org/10.1073/pnas.1320040111.

Leaf, Ryan. "Letter to My Younger Self | by Ryan Leaf." The Players' Tribune, April 26, 2017. https://www.theplayerstribune.com/articles/ryan-leaf-nfl-letter-to-my-younger-self.

Lore, Marc. "Are Your Customers in Love with You or Are You Stuck in the 'Friend Zone?'" www.yahoo.com, July 16, 2018. https://www.yahoo.com/news/customers-love-stuck-friend-zone-223846195.html.

MasterClass. "Ron Finley Teaches Gardening." MasterClass, n.d.

Miller, Lisa. "How Humans of New York Found a New Mission." Intelligencer, March 2, 2022. https://nymag.com/intelligencer/article/humans-of-new-york-brandon-stanton.html.

Pompliano, Polina. "'Atomic Habits' Author James Clear: 'I'm Never far from a Good Idea.'" theprofile.substack.com, January 12, 2021. https://theprofile.substack.com/p/james-clear?s=w.

———. "The Profile Dossier: Bryan Stevenson, the Death Row Lawyer." theprofile.substack.com, January 2, 2020. https://theprofile.substack.com/p/the-profile-dossier-bryan-stevenson.

———. "The Profile Dossier: Christina Tosi, the Chef Who Built a Dessert Empire." theprofile.substack.com, July 7, 2021. https://theprofile.substack.com/p/christina-tosi.

———. "The Profile Dossier: Marc Lore, the Serial Entrepreneur Building Billion-Dollar Companies." theprofile.substack.com, May 11, 2022. https://theprofile.substack.com/p/marc-lore.

———. "The Profile Dossier: Ron Finley, the Gangster Gardener." theprofile.substack.com, March 23, 2022. https://theprofile.substack.com/p/the-profile-dossier-ron-finley-the.

———. "The Profile Dossier: Troy Carter, Silicon Valley's Favorite Talent Manager." theprofile.substack.com, September 2, 2020. https://theprofile.substack.com/p/the-profile-dossier-troy-carter-silicon.

———. "The Profile: Why Community Is the Antidote to Loneliness." theprofile.substack.com, December 22, 2019. https://theprofile.substack.com/p/the-profile-the-billionaire-preaching?s=w.

———. "The Science behind Why Social Isolation Can Make You Lonely." theprofile.substack.com, May 9, 2020. https://theprofile.substack.com/p/the-science-behind-why-social-isolation?s=w.

Pompliano, Polina Marinova. "Inside the Mind of 'Humans of New York' Creator Brandon Stanton." theprofile.substack.com, October 20, 2020. https://theprofile. substack.com/p/inside-the-mind-of-humans-of-new.

Sacks, Danielle. "Troy Carter: Fired by Lady Gaga and Loving It." Fast Company, January 13, 2014. https://www.fastcompany.com/3024171/step-up-troy-carter.

Stevenson, Bryan. *Just Mercy: A Story of Justice and Redemption*. S.L.: Scribe Publications, 2020.

Strauss, Neil. "Elon Musk: Inventor's Plans for Outer Space, Cars, Finding Love – Rolling Stone." Rollingstone.com. Rolling Stone, November 15, 2017. https://www.rollingstone.com/culture/culture-features/elon-musk-the-architect-of-tomorrow-120850/.

Suster, Mark. "Lady Gaga's Former Mentor on Spotting, Nurturing and Mentoring Talent." Inc.com, March 1, 2016. https://www.inc.com/mark-suster/lady-gagas-former-mentor-on-spotting-nurturing-and-mentoring-talent.html.

Swift, Taylor. "Taylor Swift's Gift Giving of 2014 | SWIFTMAS." YouTube, n.d. https://www.youtube.com/watch?v=j3yyF31jbKo.

Wein, Harrison, ed. "Care and Connection." NIH News in Health, July 27, 2018. https://newsinhealth.nih.gov/2018/08/care-connection.

CHAPTER 9

arts-news 2. "Matt Haig: Reasons to Stay Alive." Vimeo, August 27, 2015. https://vimeo.com/137507982.

Brooks, David. "A Commencement Address Too Honest to Deliver in Person." The Atlantic, May 13, 2020. https://www.theatlantic.com/ideas/archive/2020/05/commencement-address-too-honest-have-been-delivered-person/611572/.

Eger, Edith Eva. *The Choice*. London: Rider, 2018.

Hartman, Darrell. "20 Odd Questions: Fashion Designer Brunello Cucinelli." *Wall Street Journal*, May 27, 2011, sec. Life and Style. https://www.wsj.com/articles/SB10001424052702304066504576341251329702820.

MasterClass. "Malcolm Gladwell Teaches Writing." MasterClass, n.d.

Murakami, Haruki. *Norwegian Wood*. Random House UK, 2013.

Musk, Elon. "Https://Twitter.com/Elonmusk/Status/1465786605889892356."Twitter, November 30, 2021. https://twitter.com/elonmusk/status/1465786605889892356.

Nielsen. "Time Flies: U.S. Adults Now Spend Nearly Half a Day Interacting with Media." Nielsen, July 2018. https://www.nielsen.com/insights/2018/time-flies-us-adults-now-spend-nearly-half-a-day-interacting-with-media/#:~:text=American%20 adults%20spend%20over%2011.

Pompliano, Polina. "'Atomic Habits' Author James Clear: 'I'm Never far from a Good Idea.'" The Profile, January 12, 2021. https://theprofile.substack.com/p/james-clear.

———. "The Profile Dossier: Brunello Cucinelli, the Philosopher King of Cashmere." theprofile.substack.com, February 24, 2021. https://theprofile.substack.com/p/ brunello-cucinelli.

———. "The Profile Dossier: Edith Eva Eger, the Holocaust Survivor Who Escaped the Prison of Her Mind." theprofile.substack.com, April 7, 2021. https://theprofile.· substack.com/p/edith-eva-eger.

———. "The Profile Dossier: Jon Kabat-Zinn, the Master of Mindfulness." theprofile. substack.com, April 27, 2022. https://theprofile.substack.com/p/jon-kabat-zinn.

———. "The Profile Dossier: Malcolm Gladwell, the Thinker Selling Good Ideas." theprofile.substack.com, May 13, 2020. https://theprofile.substack.com/p/the-profile-dossier-malcolm-gladwell?s=w.

———. "The Profile Dossier: Shonda Rhimes, the Hollywood Rule-Breaker." theprofile.substack.com, July 1, 2020. https://theprofile.substack.com/p/the-profile-dossier-shonda-rhimes.

———. "The Profile Dossier: Tom Brady, the Greatest Quarterback of All Time." theprofile.substack.com, February 3, 2021. https://theprofile.substack.com/p/tom-brady.

Rhimes, Shonda. *Year of Yes: How to Dance It Out, Stand in the Sun and Be Your Own Person.* London: Simon & Schuster UK Ltd, 2016.

Schomer, Audrey. "US Time Spent with Media 2021." Insider Intelligence, May 27, 2021. https://www.insiderintelligence.com/content/us-time-spent-with-media-2021.

Versus on Watch. "Versus on Watch - S1:E1 the Physical Game | Facebook | by versus on Watch | Coming off the Greatest Comeback in Super Bowl History, New England Patriots Quarterback Tom Brady Is Already Looking Ahead to next Season. This Premiere..." www.facebook.com, January 25, 2018. https://www.facebook.com/ vsonwatch/videos/2081108082122933/.

Wheelwright, Trevor. "Cell Phone Behavior Survey: Are People Addicted to Their Phones?" reviews.org, January 24, 2022. https://www.reviews.org/mobile/cell-phone-addiction/.

CHAPTER 10

Ballard, Chris. "David Stern Has No Time for War Stories." *Sports Illustrated*, October 24, 2018. https://www.si.com/nba/2018/10/24/david-stern-adam-silver-lebron-james-chris-paul-donald-trump-lakers-hornets.

Clear, James, and Anna Quindlen. "Redirect Notice." www.google.com, 1999. https://www.google.com/url?q=https://jamesclear.com/great-speeches/1999-mount-holyoke-commencement-speech-by-anna-quindlen.

Cole, Adam. "Does Your Body Really Refresh Itself Every 7 Years?" *NPR*, June 28, 2016, sec. Your Health. https://www.npr.org/sections/health-shots/2016/06/28/483732115/how-old-is-your-body-really.

Decent Ape. "Matthew McConaughey University of Houston Speech - YouTube." YouTube, n.d. https://www.youtube.com/watch?v=BmCTQ_mkzHU.

Hoge, Robert. "5 Things I've Learned from Being 'Ugly.'" *Time*. Accessed August 18, 2022. https://time.com/4476035/robert-hoge-advice/.

Howard, Henry. "The Running, Writing Journey of Katie Arnold." runspirited, November 26, 2019. https://www.runspirited.com/single-post/2019/11/26/the-running-writing-journey-of-katie-arnold.

Hyland, Veronique. "Dolly Parton May Look Artificial, but She's Totally Real." *Elle*, October 9, 2019. https://www.elle.com/culture/a29282948/dolly-parton-jolene-interview-2019/?.

Keown, Tim. "Francis Ngannou and His Miraculous Journey to UFC 270." ESPN.com, January 21, 2022. https://www.espn.com/espn/feature/story/_/id/33100543/francis-ngannou-miraculous-journey-ufc-stardom.

McGrath, Ben. "The Fourth Quarter." *The New Yorker*, March 24, 2014. https://www.newyorker.com/magazine/2014/03/31/the-fourth-quarter.

Morgan, Emmanuel. "The Fearsome, Quiet Champion." *The New York Times*, January 21, 2022, sec. Sports. https://www.nytimes.com/2022/01/21/sports/francis-ngannou-ufc-fight.html?utm_source=pocket_mylist.

Pompliano, Polina. "'Atomic Habits' Author James Clear: 'I'm Never far from a Good Idea.'" theprofile.substack.com, January 12, 2021. https://theprofile.substack.com/p/james-clear?r=2crk.

———. "Meet Robert Hoge, the 'Ugly' Human Living a Beautiful Life." theprofile.substack.com, August 10, 2022. https://theprofile.substack.com/p/robert-hoge-interview.

———. "Noah Galloway on Combating Depression, Building Mental Resilience, and

Starting Over." theprofile.substack.com, December 8, 2020. https://theprofile.substack.com/p/noah-galloway.

———. "The Profile Dossier: Dolly Parton, the Queen of Country Music." theprofile.substack.com, March 10, 2021. https://theprofile.substack.com/p/dolly-parton.

———. "The Profile Dossier: Kobe Bryant, Basketball's Greatest Storyteller." theprofile.substack.com, January 27, 2021. https://theprofile.substack.com/p/kobe-bryant.

———. "The Profile Dossier: Kyle Maynard, the Man Pushing the Limits of Human Potential." theprofile.substack.com, January 26, 2022. https://theprofile.substack.com/p/kyle-maynard.

———. "The Profile Dossier: Matthew McConaughey, Hollywood's 'Whiskey Philosopher.'" theprofile.substack.com, November 18, 2020. https://theprofile.substack.com/p/the-profile-dossier-matthew-mcconaughey.

———. "The Profile Dossier: UFC Champion Francis Ngannou, the Baddest Man on the Planet." theprofile.substack.com, April 13, 2022. https://theprofile.substack.com/p/francis-ngannou-ufc.

Rogan, Joe. "JRE MMA Show #99 with Francis Ngannou." open.spotify.com, February 9, 2021. https://open.spotify.com/episode/6h2N6q4gUZ32z1IsvyXFKh.

Seftel, Josh. "NOVA | ScienceNOW | Profile: Franklin Chang-Díaz: Rocket Scientist | PBS." www.pbs.org, October 2, 2008. https://www.pbs.org/wgbh/nova/sciencenow/0403/04-diaz-nf.html.

TED. "The Psychology of Your Future Self | Dan Gilbert." YouTube. Accessed August 18, 2022. https://www.youtube.com/watch?v=XNbaR54Gpj4&feature=emb_title.

CONCLUSION

Babson College. "Tory Burch's Commencement Speech at Babson College." YouTube, 2014. https://www.youtube.com/watch?v=QUjTbNcvhbY.

Burch, Tory. "Https://Twitter.com/Toryburch/Status/1261829064358268929." Twitter, May 16, 2020. https://twitter.com/toryburch/status/1261829064358268929.

Cohen, Ben. "The NASA Engineer Who Made the James Webb Space Telescope Work." *Wall Street Journal*, July 7, 2022, sec. Business. https://www.wsj.com/articles/nasa-james-webb-space-telescope-greg-robinson-images-11657137487.

Decent Ape. "Matthew McConaughey University of Houston Speech - YouTube." YouTube, n.d. https://www.youtube.com/watch?v=BmCTQ_mkzHU.

Gelles, David. "Why Melinda Gates Spends Time 'Letting My Heart Break.'" *The New*

York Times, December 4, 2020, sec. Business. https://www.nytimes.com/2020/12/04/business/melinda-gates-interview-corner-office.html.

Pompliano, Polina. "100 Couples Share Their Secrets to a Successful Relationship." theprofile.substack.com, July 16, 2020. https://theprofile.substack.com/p/100-couples-share-their-secrets-to?s=r.

———. "How to Improve Your Content Diet in the New Year." theprofile.substack.com, January 2, 2021. https://theprofile.substack.com/p/content-diet.

———. "The Profile Dossier: Grant Achatz, America's Most Creative Chef Playing Mind Games." theprofile.substack.com, September 9, 2020. https://theprofile.substack.com/p/the-profile-grant-achatz-americas?s=w.

———. "The Profile Dossier: Jerry Seinfeld, the Lifelong Student of Comedy." theprofile.substack.com, January 27, 2022. https://theprofile.substack.com/p/jerry-seinfeld.

———. "The Profile Dossier: Lionel Messi, the World's Greatest Footballer." theprofile.substack.com, June 9, 2021. https://theprofile.substack.com/p/lionel-messi.

Weiner, Jonah. "Jerry Seinfeld Intends to Die Standing Up." *The New York Times*, December 20, 2012, sec. Magazine. https://www.nytimes.com/2012/12/23/magazine/jerry-seinfeld-intends-to-die-standing-up.html?utm_source=pocket_mylist.

INDEX